ON A HIDING TO NOTHING

First Published in Great Britain in 2020 by DB Publishing, an imprint of JMD Media Ltd

ISBN 9781780916163

ON A HIDING TO NOTHING

25 YEARS AT SUNDERLAND AFC

PATRICK HOLLIS

DB PUBLISHING

CONTENTS

INTRODUCTION

Sunderland AFC were formed in 1879 by a group of schoolteachers from the town and surrounding area. The early league seasons were relatively successful, with the club enjoying a golden period in the early 20th century and winning their first FA Cup in 1937. Before this, Sunderland won the First Division title on six occasions.

After the Second World War, players who would go on to have cult hero status at Sunderland continued to come and go.

Amongst these players were Len Shackleton, Charlie Hurley and future European Cup-winning manager Brian Clough, who all turned out for Sunderland in the decades following the war.

It would be the 1970s before Sunderland next got their hands on serious silverware; and what a game it was for the club. In the 1973 FA Cup Final, there wasn't just one cult hero, there were 11. A mid-table Second Division club at the time, Sunderland overturned Leeds United, a club that were truly the team to beat in the late 1960s and early 1970s. The contest at Wembley finished 1-0 in what was an energy-sapping match.

Since that day, many things have not gone to plan for Sunderland, or have at least been more of a rollercoaster than the fans would have wanted. Most seasons ended in either relegation or promotion, with the new low of the Third Division reached with relegation in 1987.

The idea that success is usually just out of reach of Sunderland can be supported with the statistic that since 1973 Sunderland have played at Wembley on eight occasions and left empty handed from every single one. I have said many times in the past, if things click at Sunderland, they will be magical. It will happen one day, just don't ask me when.

This book looks at a small cross section of Sunderland AFC's history through the eyes of the players who represented the club. Stretching from 1984 all the way through to 2009, the players in the book talk of their time at the club and how matters on the pitch were not always how the supporters viewed them. For some, it is one of the first times they have spoken about their time at Sunderland in detail.

The players in this book have all at one point had the support of Sunderland fans everywhere. What was noticeable is that most, no matter how far away their career took them, had grown a life-long admiration for the club, the people and the city of Sunderland.

For some, this starts from keeping an eye out for the results and fortunes of their former side. For others, it comes in the form of wanting a return to Sunderland as a coach/manager to pick up from where they left off as a player.

ACKNOWLEDGEMENTS

There are people and groups who, without their support, it would not have been possible to write. First and foremost, the players who have given their time to talk to me about their time at the club. Some have spoken about their time at Sunderland more than most, but I am grateful to every player for sharing their experiences for this book.

Secondly, I would like to thank Roker Report. The online Sunderland AFC fanzine and podcast site is excellent, and it has been a pleasure to contribute for almost three years now.

More specifically, I want to thank them for putting me in contact with several of the players in this book. Without this support, the book would look far thinner with much less content. Roker Report consists of very passionate Sunderland fans and excellent content producers, both written and audio.

I would also like to thank my parents and my girlfriend for their support. I have been typing away on this book for almost two years, and it has helped to have such amazing support throughout this period.

Last, but certainly not least, I want to give thanks to DB publishing, particularly Steve and Michelle. Their support and interest in my writing has made this book.

I would also like to say thanks to A Love Supreme fanzine for agreeing to sell this book. It is much appreciated.

PART ONE
1984-1990: TO THE THIRD TIER AND BACK

The first era this book covers is one during which many local and cult heroes represented Sunderland. From the mid-80s onwards, the likes of Marco Gabbiadini, Gary Rowell, Gary Bennett and many more represented Sunderland. Some enjoyed success, but for most this came after a dark time at the club.

The mid to late 1980s was a period of firstly decline and then ascension for Sunderland. The club was relegated to Division Two at the end of the 1984-85 season, finishing 21st and losing over half of their league matches. Len Ashurst was replaced by Lawrie McMenemy in the summer, but any hopes that stability would be restored in the second tier were dashed when Sunderland finished a lowly 18th in the 1985-86 season, only to take another step back the following season and be relegated to the third tier.

It was a relegation play-off that decided Sunderland's fate, with the Black Cats drawing 6-6 on aggregate after two legs against Gillingham and going on to lose on away goals.

The time as a third-tier club would last only one season, with Sunderland storming to the title with very few hiccups along the way. Denis Smith was appointed manager at the start of this season, which was the first in a steady few years of success at Roker Park.

The 1988-89 season was one of stability, and it was needed. An uneventful 11th-place finish gave the club plenty of scope to build for a promotion push the following season. This is exactly what they did, finishing sixth and qualifying for the play-offs. A semi-final victory over the old enemy Newcastle United set up a trip to Wembley to face Swindon Town in May 1990. Despite losing on the day, events off the pitch would lead to the win being awarded to Sunderland.

This completed the bounce back from the third tier. The impact to the club of playing at its lowest level in over a century of existence didn't stay with the club like it perhaps did in 2018. The class of 1988 got the job done first time around, the class of 2018 dropped to the third tier and kept going backwards.

Unfortunately for Denis Smith's men, it was a short stay in the top tier; Sunderland were relegated at the end of the 1990-91 campaign. After this relegation you could have put your arm around a Sunderland fan to console them and said, 'Don't worry, things will get better', and you wouldn't have been lying; they would just need to endure a couple more relegations before the good times would return.

GARY BENNETT

Central-defender Gary Bennett was born in Manchester on 4 December 1961. He was first picked up by Manchester City, but it was across the border at Cardiff City where he made his first steps on to the footballing ladder.

Gary made 84 appearances and scored 11 goals for the Bluebirds, earning him a move to Sunderland in 1984. It was his manager at Cardiff, Len Ashurst, who brought Bennett to Wearside when he took over the reins at Roker Park for the start of the 1984-85 campaign. Bennett played 369 matches for Sunderland, finding the back of the net 23 times, including two minutes into his debut at Roker Park in a 3-1 victory over Southampton.

He appeared in two Wembley finals for Sunderland, unfortunately being on the losing side on both occasions in a 1-0 defeat to Norwich in the League Cup in 1985 and Liverpool in the FA Cup seven years later.

In and around the trips to Wembley, Bennett was part of promotions and relegations, including being part of the squad relegated to and then promoted from the third tier respectively in the 1986-87 and 1987-88 campaigns.

Bennett ended his 11-year stay on Wearside in 1995. In the next five years he turned out for Carlisle United, Scarborough and Darlington. As player-coach at Scarborough, he helped the side reach the Third Division play-offs in the 1997-98 campaign before Darlington had a £20,000 bid accepted for the centre-back. His playing career ended in 2002.

Standing outside the Stadium of Light press entrance before he got to work commentating on Sunderland against Stoke City in the Checkatrade Trophy, Gary first spoke of how a move to London was on the cards when he was first contacted by Sunderland.

The bright lights of London so nearly welcomed the Mancunian, as Gary said, 'I was actually on my way to Crystal Palace, that's how it all materialised. I was at Cardiff City, I worked with Len Ashurst and he left the club to take up his role at Sunderland Football Club. They were struggling at the time. When he left, he knew that my contract was up and he wanted me to go with him to Sunderland at the end of the season.'

Whilst he was anticipating a phone call from Ashurst, the South London club had stepped up their pursuit of Bennett by inviting him down to the capital. It was clear that Gary knew where he wanted his next move in the game to be, and it wasn't to London.

'Crystal Palace found out about my situation. I went down there and had talks with Steve Coppell and the chairman, then it was Ron Noades. I did agree a deal but at the back of my mind I was waiting for Sunderland to get back to me.

'At that time Sunderland were playing top-level football.'

It's something that doesn't happen often, but the allure of Sunderland playing at the highest level was partially responsible for him coming to Wearside rather than London.

Gary admitted that there was a more significant reason behind his move to Sunderland, the reason being that his manager at Cardiff had confirmed he wanted to bring him to Sunderland. Len Ashurst had worked with Gary for two years and made him one of his first-choice centre-backs at Ninian Park.

'Len had a big influence on my move to Sunderland. I played under him for two years at Cardiff and obviously top level is where everybody wants to be, playing top-level football. It was something which I couldn't really turn down.'

It was the combination of wanting to continue to work with an old manager and the chance to play First Division football that was the deal breaker for Gary. He would link up with Len Ashurst once again, and begin a spell on Wearside that would see him become a club legend.

Like most footballers who play for a club for an extended period, Gary saw his fair share of ups and downs. Arguably the lowest point in his Sunderland career, and in the club's history, was being relegated to what is now League One.

It was the first-time ever that Sunderland found themselves in the third tier of English football. The manner in which it happened saw Sunderland relegated through an old-style top and bottom play-off in the toughest way possible: away goals. The play-off saw Sunderland (third from bottom in Division Two) play Gillingham (third from top in Division Three).

Talking about this match and the importance it had for teams in two different divisions, Gary said, 'Obviously at the end of the season there was the play-off situation which I think a lot of people know about. There was a play-off at the top and a play-off at the bottom, we got involved in that, played against Gillingham, we drew 6-6 and so, in the end, we got relegated on away goals.'

Despite the relegation, Gary told of how there was no dwelling from the players and that the blue print to get promoted was drawn up almost immediately, starting with a new manager. The successful combination of experience, which Gary brought to the side, and youth was a defining factor for Gary in the success of the Third Division season.

'It was disappointing, but it was something which we had to get on with. The manager came in, Denis Smith, and he was very positive. That rubbed off on the players. He was able to put together a good squad with a mixture of youth and experience. The rest was history, everything fell into place.

'We dealt with the situation very well and there was a great feel-good factor because we were winning so many games.'

He believed Smith had the right idea from the start and that the following campaign of 1987-88 was destined to be successful, which it turned out to be. Sunderland won the title with 93 points, losing just seven of their 46 games.

In his time at the club, Gary played under several managers and admitted he got on well with all of them in one way or another. His 369 appearances for the club are a testament to how much of a professional and likeable character Gary was in the eyes of each new manager who came through the door at Roker Park.

Gary felt that he got on well with one of the more scrutinised managers in the club's history, the man who was at the helm for most of the Division Two relegation campaign in 1986-87.

'I had a good relationship with Dennis, but I had a good relationship with the majority of managers, even Lawrie McMenemy.'

Gary made a valid point that footballers often gauge their relationship on how often they get picked by whichever manager is in charge. If a player put the work in on the training ground and performed to the best of his abilities, which Gary usually did, he would make sure he was one of the first names on the team sheet.

'At the end of the day every professional footballer will feel they have a positive relationship with a manager if they are in that starting XI. That's the most important thing. That was the situation, I got on well with a lot of managers.'

He spoke often about the managers he played under, being appreciative of each one for simply having him in their plans for Sunderland, starting with the man who got Sunderland out of the third tier at the first attempt:

'Dennis was a good manager who brought a lot of success. I would say that from Len [Ashurst] all the way down to Peter Reid, who was in charge when I left, I had good relationships.'

Gary played under eight managers at Roker Park. These managers paired him with many more partners at the centre of Sunderland's defence. When talking about these players, Gary felt that each helped the side in their own way through various styles and personas.

He started with the central-defenders, who were at the club when he first joined Sunderland as a 23-year-old in 1984.

'I think they all brought different things to the table. Back when I first started, we had Gordon Chisholm and Shaun Elliot, who were both very highly thought of, both very good players, especially Shaun.

'Ian Atkins was at the football club then; you can go through a lot of players. John McPhail could do a job too, he did what he had to do. I also played along-side Andy Melville, a very good reader of the game so you know they all brought different things to the table.'

Gary was part of two cup runs for Sunderland and the one he spoke about most fondly was the 1992 FA Cup run. The final against Liverpool came after a season of relative mediocrity, finishing 18th out of 22 in Division Two.

The progress in the cup was the brightest point of an otherwise disappointing season at Roker Park. Just like in the 1973 success, Sunderland were a hot-and-cold Division Two side. The club's outstanding run saw them beat Port Vale, Oxford United, West Ham United, Chelsea and Norwich City before succumbing to Liverpool in the final.

The confidence amongst the fans after each cup match would have been sky high, yet Gary admitted that the players were down to earth and got the job done on the day, without thinking too far ahead.

'The cup is the cup. You've got, what, six rounds to play and from the very first round everyone is there hoping that they can have a good cup run. The further you go, the more the belief builds.

'That happens, not just amongst the supporters but within the group of players too. That's the same thing as what happened with us in '92. All you can do is beat what's in front of you and that's what we did; through this we managed to get to the FA Cup Final against Liverpool.'

Gary also felt lucky that he was able to feature in a cup final, pointing out that the opportunity to represent their club at Wembley is not one every player gets.

'Not many people get that chance to play in a cup final but it's one every footballer wants. I was lucky enough to get the chance against Liverpool.'

He talked more of the feeling of playing in a successful cup run, and, although the players all enjoyed it, it was a run during which the players kept focus all the way to Wembley Way.

'You go into your opening cup game and obviously you want to win it. if you do then you sit tight and see who you get in the next round. If you want the luck or to get the rub of the green, then you get a home tie and again the further you go in the competition the harder it gets.

'We had some good cup ties in the quarters and the semi-finals. We had to go down to Hillsborough and play Norwich City, it was a fantastic atmosphere, but you know as you go on you must deal with the occasion.'

About the 1992 FA Cup Final, Gary said that it could have gone either way, but unfortunately Sunderland couldn't finish their chances on the day, whereas Liverpool did.

'You need a bit of luck and someone who can put the ball in the net, which we did have with Johnny Byrne. Who knows if we could have won it? Looking back on that final it could have gone either way, especially in that first 45 minutes. Unfortunately, we didn't take our chances or opportunities, and you've got to say that after Liverpool scored early in the second half, and, in the end, they won quite comfortably.'

Gary thinks that the success of one of his former managers has only started to be appreciated in recent years. Denis Smith got Sunderland back to the First Division and took them to two Wembley finals within five years of being relegated to the third tier of English football.

He said, 'You look back at what Dennis did at that time and I think only now people are realising how good of a job he did. We needed people who would roll their sleeves up, it was important that Sunderland got promoted at the first time of asking to get back into what is now the Championship. It's the same this season [2018-19] to get out as soon as possible.'

As he was a Sunderland player for 11 years, Gary had his fair share of matches with Newcastle United. Gary may not have been a Mackem born and bred, but he certainly did more than enough to make himself an honorary citizen of Sunderland. He spoke of how the importance of playing in the derby games was made clear to him almost instantly.

'It's one thing that is drilled into you when you join Sunderland. The first thing anyone looks for is the derby games and we get told how important they are. I was lucky enough to play in at least half a dozen derbies and playing at Roker Park with its amazing atmosphere was just a fantastic occasion to be part of. If you win them it's fantastic, it's the bragging rights and we know now with the six in a row, haven't lost in the last seven. That's what the supporters live for.'

Gary said that he feels fortunate for what he has been able to do with Sunderland. He has done what every Sunderland fan would want to do, and he is one of the most respected players in the clubs history. It boiled down to a simple point for him. Gary was able to play the sport he loved at the highest level.

'When you're going into the game you want to play at the top level as much as you can. You want to be playing in front of thousands week in, week out, you want to play against the best players, win cup finals, win leagues and get promotion. When you look at it like that, for myself, I've ticked most of them boxes.

'The icing on the cake was being captain of the club, which was a fantastic highlight, and so was getting a testimonial at the club. There's lots if highs, you know. Looking back if you'd have said I would be the fifth-highest appearance maker at the club I'd have been surprised. I wouldn't change anything.'

Gary was looked upon with positivity by many of those connected with SAFC. He admitted that being involved with the club for nearly three decades and counting has made it nearly impossible to not become entirely invested.

'When you spend 11 years at a club, it's part and parcel that you fall in love with it. There will be lots of other players who would have said that, and they won't have been at the club as long as me. I've had 11 years here as a player and another 16 following the club and being part of it working for the BBC. What better job can you ask for?'

As well as the media work, Gary spoke of what he has done on the coaching side of the game since retiring in 2002. Within the coaching, there is an educational aspect that teaches respect amongst players and addresses racism within the game and wider community.

'I spent three years working in the academy at Middlesbrough. My son Andre was at the academy. I've got a coaching company set up with Julio Arca, Dean Gordon and Kieran Brady.

'That's up and running now, giving coaching and education. I've been involved with the charity 'Show Racism the Red Card', which tackles racism in society, I've been a part of that for 20 years now. I coach at the university, taking care of all the football on that side for the last 12 years. I still like to pass on my expertise to young players and to put them on the right path, so I still love to be involved on the coaching side of things.'

Gary says that he is lucky to work in the media industry with BBC Newcastle talking about a team he cares for so much:

'I'm in a privileged position. I come to work at the Stadium of Light, walk through the main entrance and see a near-enough six-foot image of myself. It doesn't get any better than that and I appreciate the football club. They have looked after me and I respect them for that. I've had a fantastic relationship with the club and that's continued. You look back and you see what you've achieved to think would you change anything? Not really no.'

He has had his critics during his co-commentary career. Often one to say exactly what he thinks and not a man to look at poor Sunderland performances through rose-tinted spectacles, Gary has always been passionate and honest when sitting in the press box.

'People say that I'm sometimes too passionate, but it's in your blood. I don't like seeing Sunderland struggle, I want to see them winning games week in, week out and in the North East football is the number-one topic, which is spoken about wherever you go and that's something you'll never get away from.

'It's difficult for supporters, including me, to walk away from. The fans stick with you through thick and thin.'

Over his years playing and talking about Sunderland, Gary has travelled the length and breadth of the country. He has been a part of some of the highest of the club's highs and the lowest of the lows.

He has nothing but praise when talking about the reaction he gets when coming across Sunderland fans.

'If you walk into Sunderland fans anywhere, not just the North East, there's an appreciation. It's something that makes you feel good.'

Gary is now a matchday institution with his media work. He is a man who cares deeply about Sunderland Association Football Club and he will no doubt be a part of the fabric of the matchday experience for many more years to come.

PAUL LEMON

Paul Lemon was born in Middlesbrough, but it was with Sunderland that he signed his first professional contract. Whilst at Roker Park, he went out on loan to Carlisle United, Walsall, Reading and Chesterfield. The latter he left for permanently in 1993. The bulk of his appearances may have been made over just two seasons, but these campaigns saw Sunderland drop into the Third Division for the first time in their history and then win the league at a canter at the first attempt.

A centre-forward by trade, Paul was often utilised as a right-sided winger, and during the Third Division title-winning season of 1987-88 he found the back of the net nine times, helping Sunderland to return to the second tier of English football in some style. Injury cut Paul's career short at the age of 27, but his time at Sunderland enabled him to show the Roker Park faithful a glimpse of his full potential.

As mentioned, Paul was very young when he joined Sunderland. In fact, he was a 14-year-old schoolboy when he signed on the dotted line at Roker Park. 'I signed up as a schoolboy and then when I left school aged 16 I signed as an apprentice. I did my two years of apprenticeship then signed pro.'

His move to Sunderland, however, almost didn't happen. Representatives of his home-town club were more than on his doorstep at one point in his early life: 'The chief scout at Middlesbrough was in my room with the papers out ready to sign and, for some reason, I didn't sign them. Looking back in hindsight, I probably would have now as they were my home team.' Middlesbrough weren't the only team in the running for Paul's signature. 'I went to look at Sunderland, Aston Villa and Manchester City before deciding on Sunderland.' It was one man who seemingly had at least some influence on Paul's final decision: 'I joined Sunderland and at the time the youth team was coached by Jim Montgomery. When you meet the guy and, to see how he's a great coach and a good guy, it just made my mind up. he was superb to me.''A guy called Peter Eustace was there as youth-team coach, and with Jim Montgomery as well. I was fortunate enough to play in the FA Youth Cup when I was still at school, so I'd already had an inkling of what was going to happen. We got to the semi-final of that cup and along the way I was having to get time off school to go and play, it was fantastic. We played the semi-final at Roker Park and the referee told us half an hour before kick-off that we had to delay it because there were that many people trying to get into the match. The fan base has always been there, even at youth level.'Paul admitted that when he first started playing his young age helped to cope with the daunting environment of professional football. 'It was difficult at first when we were in the First Division. When you're a 17/18-year-old lad like I was you just play with no fear. You don't really take the crowd and the atmosphere in, it's only when you're older that you start looking at the crowd and thinking that you'll make mistakes, but in the early days you just play with no fear.'

The biggest of matches for Sunderland players are usually against Newcastle. Paul didn't really take note of the full house at Roker Park until he was off the pitch some years later: 'I played in the Sunderland-Newcastle match in 1984 in the First Division and there were over 30,000 there, you just don't notice it until afterwards.' Most players, past and present, have opinions on supporters of the clubs they once played for. Paul is no exception; he gave a more honest opinion than many. 'With Sunderland fans it's a flip of the coin and that's not being nasty, they are superb, if everything is going well. Equally, it's tough if things aren't going to plan. Generally, though, they are fantastic.' It was clear to me that, despite not having the longest spell on Wearside, his time at the club obviously meant a great deal to him.

Our conversation moved on towards a period of Paul's career at Sunderland which many fans won't remember fondly. He played a significant part in the club's Third Division campaign of 1987-88, but it was the previous season that we spoke about first and he told me what the mood was like around the dressing room as Sunderland were relegated from the second tier of English football: 'It goes back to when I was a younger player. I was 21/22 in that Second Division season and had I been older I would have had a different slant on it.

I was interested to know if Paul had an idea of what went wrong in that relegation season, and it seemed simple enough in all honesty: 'We just didn't gel that year, but from my point of view there was no animosity in the dressing room. It just didn't happen, we didn't sulk about it and you know Dennis came in and cheered the place up with the training methods. From then on, we rolled our sleeves up and during the next season we never looked back. What happened, happened and we just got on with it. we got the club back where it belonged.'

Scoring goals was what Paul felt he was in the side for, being an attacking player. He understandably treasured all the goals he scored for Sunderland, but there was a tinge of light-hearted frustration that a couple of his best goals weren't more high profile: 'If you ask any professional footballer which goal stands out the most they'll say all of them stand out. There isn't one that really sticks out. My two best goals never get talked about because they were against Scarborough away from home in the Football League Trophy. One was a left foot and one was a chip over the keeper. They don't get mentioned as it was just one of those silly trophy games, there's a bit more prestige in that competition now. I've never seen any footage since of those goals, but they were two of my favourites.' He enjoyed these goals and he seemed grateful for every occasion he hit the back of the net. 'Every goal is a special goal. Whether it's from 30 yards or a tap in.' Paul did narrow down the subject a little further, telling me that goals at one end of Roker Park were always to be remembered. Even more so, the occasion when he scored past the most expensive goalkeeper at that time. 'Every goal kicking towards the Fulwell End would be special. I keep getting reminded that I scored against Nigel Martyn, who was the first million-pound goalkeeper. It's not until people tell you those stats that you realise what it's all about.'

Paul seemed to relish hearing about those stats once hanging up his boots, but at the time those things weren't on his mind.

Denis Smith was the man tasked with getting Sunderland out of the third tier of English Football in the 1987-88 season. Paul believed that he came into the club with an only-way-is-up attitude, he brought the sort of positive vibe to the club that had been lacking. 'You can look at it and say there's only one way this club is going to go and that's up. That's what happened, the mood from him was just so upbeat but then is was also serious.' Paul remembered how Smith had the team working hard on the pitch but off it he made sure there was at least some element of relaxation.

'Training had good intensity but once you stopped training you were chilled, and everyone was joking. We all went away together, on trips and stuff like that. The bond between the squad was the same after relegation as it was before.' Despite what the fans might have thought, Paul was confident in saying that the mood in the dressing room didn't change much despite the relegation to Division Three.

He also felt there was a significant difference in the training techniques of Denis Smith and one of his predecessors: 'Training was much more enjoyable under Smith, that's nothing against Lawrie [McMenemy] or anyone else, but it was more enjoyable under Dennis. I think that was testament to his personality, it shone through to us.'Paul obviously thoroughly enjoyed his time playing at Roker Park but through his eyes things started to come apart relatively quickly once he departed the club: 'This attitude came with us onto the pitch and into the following season following promotion from the third tier, we did quite well if I remember rightly. Unfortunately, though, we couldn't kick on after that and I left for Chesterfield.

Even though he'd left the club by the time Smith was sacked as Sunderland manager, Paul was quick to appreciate what he did for Sunderland and how the fans would have noticed how well he did under testing circumstances. 'Denis got the sack as well, so I'm not sure what happened, but I'm sure the Sunderland fans recognised how good of a job he did.'Paul played alongside several players who became cult heroes on Wearside; however, he never viewed any of these players as role models. Opposition players were a different matter, however. 'The opposition offered up players. There was never any one player who I thought to myself, "I want to be like you," but there were plenty of players I played against who made me consider that. Peter Beardsley and even Eric Gates when we went and played at Ipswich.' Paul would have played alongside Eric Gates on many an occasion in red and white, but he felt he noticed the quality he possessed when being on opposite sides.

Paul experienced the true footballing fairy tale from being a fan and then a player, taking him closer to players he idolised whilst watching Middlesbrough. 'One thing that does stick in my mind was getting picked up from Middlesbrough for training with my boyhood heroes Dave Hodgson and Mark Proctor. Not to say I'd want to play football like them, but they were two players I looked up to. I'd gone from watching them from the terraces as they played for Middlesbrough to training with them as a team-mate at Sunderland.'What was certain was that Paul felt his time at Sunderland never properly reached expectations. 'I always say this to people now, including Sunderland fans. I never showed my true potential at Sunderland. I don't know why I didn't, it's just one of these things that happened.'

He felt that not being played in a familiar position on the pitch, his pace on the wing helped see to that and could be viewed as a setback for his hopes of being played in his desired role. 'All I can say is that I grew up playing up front, I got my apprenticeships playing upfront and suddenly when I turned 18 I was playing regularly in the first team on wide-right midfield. I was never a midfield player, but I was put there as I had an eye for goal and I could get up and down the pitch very easily.'Paul was always proud of how hard he worked on the pitch and he assured that it was something Sunderland fans could have no issue with: 'One thing Sunderland fans can't have a go at me for is lack of effort. I never left anything on the pitch, but I often look back and think I didn't really do myself justice playing wide-right-midfield. I wish I had the chance to play up front more, but Gazza and Gatesy [Gary Rowell and Eric Gates] were such a phenomenal pairing it would have been impossible to break through.

'Yet I do wish I'd been given the chance to play off them or around them, but we played 4-4-2 and I was right-midfield and that was it for all my days at Sunderland. A little bit of regret there but that's just the way it goes.'Football can be a game of fortune and Paul felt that he made his breakthrough into the Sunderland first team at an unlucky time. His ambition to play upfront was always going to be challenged by the fact he had two of the best strikers in the club's history to compete with. The timing wasn't great, but it was clear he still enjoyed being in the squad despite being played on the wing more than he would have wanted.

'They were a fantastic pairing, but no 18-year-old lad is going to say, "No I'm not playing outside-right I want to play in my position or not play at all". I was picked to play in that position and I did it. At the time I never really whinged, it's only when I've looked back at my career that I've wished I'd have been given a chance to play upfront. I scored goals for the youth and reserve teams, would I have been able to continue that in the first team? Well we'll never know, but if I could get goals from midfield then I'm sure I could have got them from upfront as well. That's just the way the managers see it and you just must get on with it.'

Paul wasn't bitter, his ability was recognised, it was just that he was up against two prolific centre-forwards at the time.

His career at Sunderland never really got going and others may have regretted that; however, Paul said that he wouldn't change anything about the way his career played out. The benefit of hindsight was important for Paul.

'It's not until you finish the professional game that you look back and think, "I wish I'd been able to play in that position", because even when I went to Chesterfield I played midfield, then I got my injury which was the end of it. In three seasons at Chesterfield I only managed to play around two because I was out for a year. You can look back on life and wish things could be different but at the time you just get on with it.' Living and working in Sunderland helped Paul to understand what the city and its football team was all about. Paul said he wouldn't change a thing: 'I'd probably do the same again if given the opportunity, I'd play where I was told to. I'd imagine these days players have a bit more power. We were brought up to play football. Yes, I'm from Middlesbrough, but I understood the Sunderland fans' passion. We lived in the hostel on the sea front there, I stayed there for two years so I knew what it meant to the fans to be there. I did try, some people liked it, and some didn't. That's just the way it goes.' Despite the lack of opportunities in his favoured position, Paul was confident in saying that he enjoyed his time on Wearside. Granted, it wasn't the best period in the club's history. However, he contributed more than most in the Third Division campaign of 1987-88. He did note that the fans had the tendency to make their feelings towards him known, yet at such a tough time for the club he would hardly have been the only one.

'Loved it, I loved it. Yeah there were times when the fans got on my back but I always tried to work my hardest and in general the fans were brilliant with me. It was a tough time for the club but after we were relegated we rolled our sleeves up, got on with it and bounced back. I'm quite proud that I got to be part of that.' I felt it was testament to his character that he showed pride during his time at the club at a point when things weren't going to plan at Roker Park.

Injury cut Paul's career short, but he found himself spending most of his life afterwards dedicated to football in other ways, after a short stay in a financial role. 'I did my cruciate ligament at Chesterfield and when I finished in 93/94 you didn't have the academy set up which is around now, so jobs in football were scarce. I took a different attitude, I went into the financial world, but I left that a few years back.

He kept his foot in the footballing door through training but his true calling in the game came through a different avenue. I took my coaching badges purely because I enjoyed the coaching side of it, I coached some local kids. Then I bumped into my old colleague at Chesterfield, a guy called Lee Turnbull.

He was head of recruitment at Huddersfield in 2013, and I basically asked him what opportunities were out there and he said well I can't help you there, but he did have a vacancy in the scouting department. That was my first foot in and since then I've worked at Huddersfield, Sheffield United, Wigan and Scunthorpe for the last two and a half seasons.' His role at these clubs has been something which Paul spoke of with such passion, 'I love it, my responsibilities are to get out and watch the opposition quite a lot. This includes looking at how the side set up, strengths and weaknesses, things like that. These reports go to the analysis guys and then the manager to pick the bones out of it and use what they can for the upcoming match. They present it to the lads but only some basic information. I've been doing that for the last six years. I love it, getting out to report on players and performances. It's not the same as playing or being involved with coaching but it's the next best thing.'

Going around the grounds and giving his views on opposition players is his game now.

Paul continued to talk about his role as a scout, telling of who he ends up meeting on his often long-distance travels. 'You meet your ex-colleagues on the way. I've bumped into Gordon Armstrong, Gary Rowell, and Malcolm Crosby recommended me for a role at Wigan Athletic so that was great. I've bumped into a few ex-Sunderland lads and there's a few who I'd like to again.' His career at Sunderland might not have played out exactly how he wanted, but Paul only had one regret and it was one which undoubtedly almost any Sunderland player would have. 'They are all good memories of Sunderland. It's a great club, my biggest regret though would be not being able to play at the Stadium of Light. What an honour that would have been. Why would anyone not want to play in front of 30,000 at that ground? Opposition players just up their game. It's a chance I would have loved to have had.'

Paul continues to work as a scout and this takes him up and down the land to grounds of all shapes and sizes. He came up through the Sunderland youth system and was confident that he always worked very hard for the fans. At any other time, Paul could have been Sunderland's leading centre-forward. As it was, he was asked to play on the wing. Being a young player eager for first-team football, Paul stepped up to the mark. To some extent, his career is a case of what could have been. Injury brought his playing days to a premature end, but off the pitch Paul has been able to continue to contribute to English football. He may be coming to scout at a football ground near you soon.

REUBEN AGBOOLA

Reuben Agboola was born in Camden, North London, in 1962. He signed for Southampton as a youth player in 1978, signing as a professional two years later. His time at Southampton came to an end in 1985, as he was signed for Sunderland by Len Ashurst. A full-back by trade, Reuben made over 150 appearances for Sunderland and experienced the highs and lows that few players have.

When he left Sunderland in 1991, Reuben had become a household name around the area and left with a Third Division title under his belt. Whilst at Sunderland, he was on loan at Charlton Athletic and Port Vale, but his permanent move from Roker Park took him to Swansea City.

Whilst at the Swans, Reuben made just short of 30 appearances. In 1993 he moved to Woking, ending his career with Gosport Borough.

Before signing for Sunderland, Reuben had made himself a regular at The Dell for Southampton. This was mainly because of him being able to play successfully in a sweeper role, along with energy and tenacity.

It wasn't always so straightforward, and Reuben was initially thrown into a Southampton side that was plagued with injury, only to later lose his place once more.

In a true turn of strange coincidence, Reuben was made to wait for his debut for Sunderland. He featured in a match against Liverpool on 12 January 1985; however, this was abandoned, and his official debut came against former club Southampton. The match at his old stomping ground was won by the hosts 1-0 and Sunderland ended the 1984-85 season in the Division One relegation zone.

Despite signing in 1985, it wouldn't be until the 1987-88 campaign in the third tier of English football where Reuben would lock down a place in the side. A fan favourite at the club, Reuben would go on to become the first African player to pick up an international cap whilst at Sunderland, when Nigeria selected him in 1990.

The season Reuben signed on Wearside, Sunderland took part in what would be their first of three Wembley finals in the space of seven years. The 1985 League Cup Final ended in a 1-0 defeat for Sunderland, with Reuben being unable to play due to being cup tied. This was after appearing for Southampton earlier in the competition.

When asked about how the move to Sunderland came about and how he ended up swapping the south coast of England for the North East, Reuben explained that it was a footballing stalwart who had played for and coached over half a dozen teams through an illustrious career.

'Frank Burrows was the man who sold the idea to me. I liked his honesty, he thought I could stabilise the defence.'

Suring up the defence was something that Sunderland were in desperate need for. In Reuben's first season at the club, they had shipped over 60 goals. The previous season, this number was 52. Conceding goals would remain an issue for Sunderland until the Third Division promotion campaign, a season which the club dominated and bounced back into the Second Division at the first time of asking.

To go back to the stats, Sunderland conceded 48 goals in 46 matches and lost just seven of these.

Sunderland may not have been the only club interested in Reuben's signature in 1985, but he couldn't have been certain due to the tight-lipped nature of then Southampton manager and future Sunderland boss Lawrie McMenemy.

When asked if other teams wanted to sign him, Reuben said that McMenemy never mentioned any; however, the former Nigerian international considered this may have been because his manager wanted to make sure the deal benefitted himself and Southampton.

He said, 'There were no other teams, not that I know of. McMenemy wasn't big on the truth, so it usually meant you went where he got the best deal for himself or he'd have you playing with the juniors.'

For Sunderland fans, Reuben will be best remembered as a full-back who was able to slot in at the centre of the defence when it was required of him. However, he explained that he had played in many other positions during his career, the sweeper role at Southampton being one of the most successful during this time.

'I played every position at Southampton in the reserves, even centre-forward. Then I established myself in the sweeper role after playing in midfield or full-back in home matches and sweeper in away matches. I finally ended up playing right or left-back and centre-half at Sunderland.'

As he was perhaps underutilised until the Third Division campaign, Reuben felt that it was an enjoyable experience being a major player in the title success.

It was during this season that Denis Smith took over at Roker Park after the departure of McMenemy, a manager Reuben felt constantly overlooked him.

'It was out of my control as far as relegations were concerned, but as the record books say I played most of my football getting back into the First Division. Yes, it was satisfying coming back up and disappointing that I was overlooked until after McMenemy left.'

In comparison to some players at the club during the Third Division promotion season, Reuben was a seasoned professional. For many, it was their first season at the club and for others they were still fresh to the professional game. Amongst these were Gary Owers and Paul Lemon, who have also shared their thoughts on their respective Sunderland careers in this book.

On the squad at the beginning of that season, Reuben felt that, due to the lack of resources available to a third-tier team in 1987, the management at Sunderland had a plan and they stuck to it. As it turned out, this plan was hugely successful and propelled Sunderland into a period of improvement, which saw them reach the FA Cup Final and get promoted to the First Division by 1992.

He said, 'I don't think they had the time or resources to overhaul the squad. They brought in some youth and it was all about getting the best out of what you had and then see what improvements could be made.'

Reuben added that one of the most influential players and biggest characters in the dressing room was Eric Gates, another player who would become a cult hero at Roker Park. His nod for best manager during his time at the club would be expected when you glance back at his history at Sunderland, but Reuben was still complimentary of Denis Smith. Many have said that Smith's spell at Sunderland was under-rated. When you look at what he did with limited resources, there is a good argument for this.

Reuben, along with Eric and Denis, were all in St James' Park on one spring night in 1990 when a memorable away-day victory over the old enemy was achieved. The 1990 Division Two play-offs would ultimately be remembered for Swindon's 1-0 victory over Sunderland, but Sunderland's ultimate promotion due to the Robins' financial irregularities.

Yet the semi-final second leg between Newcastle United and Sunderland at St James' will always be remembered for the right reasons by Mackems up and down the land. After a cagey 0-0 draw at Roker Park, it was winner takes all on Tyneside. Sunderland went into enemy territory and came back with the goods: a place at Wembley in the play-off final. Eric Gates and Marco Gabbiadini scored one each in a 2-0 victory.

Reuben thoroughly enjoyed his time on Wearside and felt as though the club had both under and over-achieved during this period.

Leaving for Swansea City in November 1991, Reuben ended a period of relative success at Sunderland. When he joined, the club was on a downward trajectory towards what was then the lowest league season in its history. He left the north east of England with Sunderland back in the First Division and within months of only their fourth FA Cup Final. The 1992 final appearance is still the last time Sunderland have reached Wembley in the famous competition.

Reuben would move on out of the game after hanging up his boots for good later in the decade. He gave an insight into what he has done since retiring, and how the influence of a brewery native to Sunderland helped to get him to pursue a career in pub ownership.

A staple of the North East, Vaux Breweries sponsored the football club for an extended period, some of these years coming during Reuben's time at Sunderland. Reuben said that this is where his first post-retirement occupation sprang from.

'I got involved in Vaux Breweries whilst at Sunderland, so I spent ten years in the licensed trade running a pub. I left the licensed trade in 2004 and I have been involved in the car trade ever since.

Reuben started his youth career and then his professional footballing career on the Hampshire coast at Southampton. He moved from Sunderland to South Wales, with loan spells at Charlton Athletic and Port Vale in between. Despite the travelling, it was Southampton where he has since made his home. As is the case with so many other former Sunderland players, the club has stuck with Reuben.

To this, he added, 'Although I still live in Southampton, Sunderland still remains a big part of my life.'

When asked to give a summary of his time at Sunderland and his six years at Roker Park, Rueben's reply was simple yet effective.

He said, 'Ha'way the lads.'

Reuben Agboola was one of the rare group of players who, before the club's relegation in 2018, had represented Sunderland at the lowest level in the club's history. It was a dark time for Sunderland Association Football Club, but so many of the players who represented the club during that season owned the shirt.

Some went on to bigger and better clubs, others stuck by the team and helped them into the First Division once again. Reuben was one of the latter, arguably playing some of his best and most consistent football during a spell which many Sunderland supporters may want to forget.

He was undoubtedly a positive to come out of that season, and the interest and passion Reuben still shows about the club is evidence that he still very much cares about Sunderland.

GARY OWERS

Born in Newcastle in 1968, Gary Owers was signed up to Sunderland as a schoolboy when he was 15. Making his debut in 1986, Gary went on to enjoy eight years at Roker Park, playing well over 300 times for Sunderland.

The midfielder departed Wearside in 1994 for Bristol City, where he spent four years and racked up over 100 appearances. The ever-presence of Gary carried over into his next club, with him playing over 150 times for Notts County from 1998 through to 2002. His last club as a full-time player was then-Conference side Forest Green Rovers, a club he would later manage.

Gary gained coaching and managerial experience at the Gloucestershire club as well as Bath, Plymouth Argyle, Aldershot Town, Gateshead and Torquay United.

Going back to his move to Sunderland, Gary explained what it was like to join the club and how the life of a youth player at a football club was very different in the 1980s compared to now. This was mainly in the sense of the expansive youth academy or youth leagues.

'I signed schoolboy forms when I was 15, that would have been around 1984. I was going to Lord Lawson School in Birtley then. You didn't really play games then like you do now from an early age, you sort of just trained a few times a week.

'We obviously had a youth team, but when you're 15 you'd have a couple of games at the end of the season. It was like a trial really, to see if you were up to moving into the youth team the next season as an apprentice.'

He is a local to the North East, but Gary said that sides elsewhere in the country were interested in his signature. He added that he was at Middlesbrough at the same time as one of the most iconic players in England's recent history.

'I went on trial to Notts County, who were in the higher divisions then, Coventry, Middlesbrough. I was on trial at Middlesbrough when Paul Gascoigne was there, that was entertaining, even at that age. He had no kit, no boots and would manage to blag himself into getting them.

'Norwich were interested too, but when Sunderland showed an interest Joe Church, who was youth development officer, pretty much said he wanted me to sign. I was offered schoolboy forms, I lived in Birtley and was training in Washington, so I was more than happy to sign.'

It was Denis Smith who gave Gary his first-team debut, but it was Smith's predecessor who had provided Gary with the opportunity to become a professional player at Sunderland.

'I'd done two years as an apprentice and Lawrie McMenemy, before he left, had offered me a two-year professional contract, I was very fortunate really to get that offer. Then Denis Smith came in and put me straight into the team.'

Smith led Sunderland during a relatively successful period for the club, and Gary spoke of his relationship with the man who would lead Sunderland to two promotions during his tenure. He also added how Smith had been interested in taking him to York City on loan whilst he was manager at Bootham Crescent.

'It was excellent. He knew who I was. You go into training on the first day as a professional with a new manager who you want to try and impress. Both him and Viv, even the fact that they knew my name meant something to me.

'As time wore on, he said that he had been trying to sign me on loan when he was at York. This is when I was still a youth player at Sunderland, so he'd known who I was for a while.'

Gary talked through his progress from signing as a schoolboy: 'I got involved in all the pre-season games before that season and then I was straight in the first team for the opening league match at Brentford.

'You knew of the first team players, what used to happen was the youth team used to get changed in the away team dressing room as well as the reserves. So, you feel quite confident in there, you're with your mates working, training and living together, we used to live in a hostel on the seafront at Roker which was a lot of fun.'

The step up in the squad from a youth player to senior was explained by Gary through the transition from being in one dressing room and then stepping up to the first team set up across the way at Roker Park.

'As you get elevated up the pecking order you need to walk into the professional dressing room. There's one or two lively characters that want to put you in your place, so you sort of go in and keep your head down at first. I had a peg next to Eric Gates and Reuben Agboola, so I was quite happy there. They were both good blokes, good players, good pros and particularly Eric, I was under his wing for a bit when I first started.'

Eric Gates is a player who was a household name for many Sunderland fans and, for a certain generation, always will be. One half of a formidable strike force in the 1980s and 1990s along with Marco Gabbiadini, Eric was a regular on the score sheet at Sunderland. He was also a near-perfect role model for a young Gary Owers to have in his first season as a professional.

Gary's first campaign as a first-team player was Sunderland's first in the third tier of English football. He explained what it was like to watch the team struggle from the side-lines and to then ultimately be given the nod as one of the players tasked with getting the club bouncing back at the first time of asking.

Gary said that Lawrie McMenemy had tried and failed to repeat a blueprint which had given him success elsewhere in the footballing world.

'What happened over the summer was that Lawrie had tried to repeat the formula he had at Southampton by signing players who were towards the end of their careers but were still good players and it just hadn't worked out for them elsewhere.

'A lot of them had left, it was a fresh start and there were fewer of those faces around at the start of the season, and one or two younger lads had been moved up from the youth team. It was a professional first-team dressing room.

'I had been an apprentice, watched the team struggle and get relegated, there was devastation. It was the first time Sunderland had ever been in the third tier. Massive club and we had to get out as quickly as possible. Thankfully, Denis came in and we did it at the first time of asking.'

It may have been the club's lowest point in its history, but Sunderland stumbled a few times on the way to the Third Division title. Gary said that the positivity which was bred out of this season propelled himself and the team forward in the seasons to come.

'The winning mentality of the Third Division season was a benefit for the next few seasons. Denis turned it around quickly. We were in the Third Division; we couldn't have done any better. We were there to be shot at, the big team in the league with the big crowds. We got turned over a few times, I remember a 4-0 defeat at Bristol Rovers, but we got through.

'I remember the following season in Division Two we were quite comfortable in mid-table before the following season getting into the play-offs and then into the top division. We did have two or three seasons of success to go from the Third Division to the top division, even though we were slightly fortunate with what happened to Swindon Town at the time.'

The 1990 Second Division play-off final might not sound like the most stand-out of Wembley finals in the past decades, yet the 1-0 victory for Swindon over Sunderland would go down as one of controversy. Despite the victory, Swindon were later found guilty of financial irregularities and promotion was awarded to Sunderland.

Gary was a key player during the season and the play-off final itself. He spoke of how it felt to go from the lows of a Wembley defeat to the highs of promotion.

'It was strange emotionally. We ended the season on a high, in great form, especially away from home. we had some great victories. I remember on the Bank Holiday weekend we went to Port Vale and Wolves, winning back-to-back games. We stayed over at Keele University and had a great weekend.

'Then you're gearing up for the final against Swindon, obviously on the back of one of the biggest and best derby victories at St James' Park. We were full of confidence. I wouldn't say we felt invincible, but we didn't think we could be beaten.'

Gary held his hands up by saying Sunderland were second best on the day, and that Swindon's fortune was the only way they could have scored past an excellent goalkeeping display by Tony Norman in the Sunderland goal.

'When we got to Wembley, we were beaten by a better team on the day. Swindon were excellent, they should have won the game easily. It ended up being a scrappy, deflected goal which won it in the end. It was from outside the box, the deflection took it past Tony Norman. I think that's the only way Swindon would have scored that day because Tony Norman was outstanding.'

As Gary went on, the few days from the final defeat and finding out they would be a First Division team after all was a true rollercoaster of emotion for Sunderland players, as it likely was for the fans.

'We came off the pitch totally dejected. We'd been through a long season and finished on a low. A couple of days later we got the call and it sunk in that we were going to be promoted, which was unbelievable really. We were able to enjoy it.'

Gary said that the issue of what happened with Swindon Town was unfortunate for the Football League, but one which Sunderland without a doubt benefitted from.

'It was rumbling on and spoke about. We weren't going into the final thinking whatever happens we're going to get promoted, not by any means. Nobody knew really, it was something new in football.

'I think it was a big embarrassment for the Football League at the time. They had to deal with Swindon, of course the ideal scenario for us was that we played the game at Wembley and beat Swindon. We had to deal with it in a different way.

'Of course, Swindon won on the day, but I think initially they were relegated two divisions because of what happened. That was overturned though; however, we reaped the benefit of that decision and got promoted. I think we were in a pub somewhere celebrating promotion only days after losing a final at Wembley.'

It's fair to say few teams have been able to go to the pub in the circumstances which the 1989-90 Sunderland squad found themselves under. The players were catapulted from the deflating feeling of falling at the last promotion hurdle, to then looking forward to playing against the likes of Arsenal, Liverpool and Manchester United.

Fast forward two years and Sunderland are a hit-and-miss First Division team who have enjoyed a swashbuckling FA Cup run, with the Black Cats getting to the 1992 final to face Liverpool.

When asked if the cup run was a benefit to the club's league form, Gary said, 'It was the opposite really. We were poor, we nearly got relegated if I remember rightly. Denis had left, that was disappointing, Malcolm had come in as caretaker. We started getting the results in the cup, that helped his cause in getting the job permanently, it was unbelievable.'

Gary played a role in Sunderland's first and last matches on the cup run, but it was a frustrating campaign for him.

'On a personal level, I played in the third round and had a bad injury and ended up missing all of the other rounds up until the final. I was lucky that I got the opportunity to play in the final, I was able to play in the last few games of the season.

'I probably put myself into the reckoning just by being out on the pitch, you look at the lads who were in the team. John Byrne had done really well, as had Brian Atkinson and Paul Bracewell. I'm looking at players like that and thinking, "I could play ahead of you". Possibly if John Kay hadn't been injured, I wouldn't have featured.'

The benefits of a good, old-fashioned FA Cup run are perhaps overlooked by many teams in the current era, but Gary said that there was little that could knock the spirit of the players during the run with everyone travelling, even those who were out of action through injury.

'The spirit in the camp was brilliant. We all travelled to the games, I did even when I was injured. The West Ham game away from home was unbelievable. The performance on the night was outstanding, and then everyone will remember the Chelsea game at Roker Park and Gordon Armstrong's diving header to win that one. Those are the moments which stand out.

'At the end of the previous season we felt a bit like that, where we were always going to win, especially away from home. You get that feeling that you're going to win games, and that's what happened to the lads. They got on a roll and it took us all the way to the final.'

Gary got on well with most of his team-mates at Sunderland, including a midfield partner whom he stayed with for a time whilst at the club.

'For different reasons, Eric took me under his wing and then Paul because I started playing alongside him in midfield. He looked after me off the pitch as well, I spent a short period of time staying with him and his wife.

'I also had relationships; we were friends with other players. This happened with

Gordon Armstrong, Dickie Ord, they were my mates. We played in the youth team and then the reserves. Other people in the squad, John Cornforth he was a young player as well who didn't play every week but was around the squad.'

The amount of time spent together outside of the confines of the training ground helped to create a strong bond between the players, according to Gary.

'We had a close bond. We spent a lot of time in each other's company, we would socialise together and go away on trips abroad during and after the season. This, plus staying together in hotels overnight for away games, helped us to be very close throughout the season.'

A successful couple of years on the pitch had Sunderland fans enjoying the game again after a poor run during the mid-1980s. Gary spoke of how these seasons were both successful and enjoyable.

'We had three or four really good years. If you think we won the Third Division, got promoted from the Second Division and then played in a cup final whilst being a First Division club. We'd had a good period in the grand scheme of things. I'm still close now to a lot of those people I have spoken about.'

Gary's time at Sunderland came to an end after eight years as a reliable and key member of the squad. Although he said it felt right at the time, Gary has since looked back and wished he had ridden out a tough period emotionally and stay at the club beyond 1994.

'It came to a natural end. However, looking back, I don't think I should have. At that point in time I needed to get away. I'd had a bad couple of years off the pitch. My mother passed away when I was young, that had a massive impact on the family, and one or two other things had built up. I just felt I needed to get away and start afresh. I wish I had stuck it out, I think the biggest disappointment in my life was leaving Sunderland and never getting the chance to go back and play against them.

'When it did happen, it happened very quickly. It was very close to Christmas, we'd played Bristol City on the Saturday and I didn't think for one second I would be playing for Bristol City the next week against somebody else; I think it was West Brom who I played my first match against.'

A regret from Gary was that he didn't stay at Sunderland, but at the time it felt right to leave Wearside.

'It never crossed my mind. I was young, I didn't have an agent and I didn't really have anyone to talk it through with. I had to make the decision myself and I should have waited until at least the end of the season.

'Things might have been different obviously if I had hung around, Reidy seemed to pick things up quick. He hit the ground running, he got that team spirit going, which was key for our success, and will be at any football club. Where any team has success, it will be built around having a good, healthy team spirit. It was a sad time really.'

Reflecting on his time at Sunderland, Gary had nothing but praise for the side. He was keen to point out his impressive achievement of playing well over 300 times and had several achievements under his belt by the time he was just 25, a tally which would rarely be seen in the current climate.

'None of the clubs I played for after Sunderland were as big as Sunderland, in that context in terms of support. People don't realise, I was only 25 when I left. I'd played over 320 league and cup games, had two promotions, played in a play-off final and FA Cup Final, so I'd done a lot quite early. I don't know if I maybe took some of that for granted because it happened to me so early.

'In terms of being a professional, you get older and your body changes physically, and athletically you can't do what you once were able to do once upon I time.'

Gary talked of his career after he left Sunderland, highlighting that he was a familiar name on the team sheet wherever he went.

'I played for some good managers, such as Joe Jordan at Bristol City and Sam Allardyce at Notts County. Most of the time I was fit, I got selected. I never had niggly injuries, when I was injured it was usually quite serious. When I sit at the end of it, I carried on playing until I was 34, I won a promotion with Bristol City. I didn't really win anything at Notts County, but I was there a few seasons and I was an ever-present.'

He feels a sense of pride at what he achieved, racking up a number of career appearances that he feels he would manage as regularly in the modern game.

'Whatever I did at the end of it, I finished with something like 600 league and cup appearances. That's not to be sniffed at and it's something which I am proud of. Not many people play over 500 league games, especially now in the modern game where players get rested and rotated. The best, most exciting and successful part of my career was without a doubt at Sunderland.'

Gary's transition from a player into a coach began at Bath City and has seen him travel up and down the land in various job roles. He gave an insight into what this part of his career has been like so far.

'I've worked at Portsmouth when they were in the Premier League, the FA Cup Final and during their time in Europe, I ran a massive football development programme there. I've worked for the FA, I've been a coach educator, manager, assistant manager, head of coaching, head of academy, chief scout, head of recruitment. I've had many roles in football.

'In terms of being successful, I went to Walsall with Kevin Dillon who is another Sunderland lad. He played for Newcastle but was always a big Sunderland fan. Looking back, we were able to get Aldershot, who were unfashionable at the time, into the play-offs to get into League One from League Two. That was their highest league finish at that point, when you look at where they are now it was a significant achievement.'

Gary has played his part in the odd great escape as an assistant manager, including one job down on the south coast in Devon.

'The jobs I've had in management or as an assistant manager have usually been at the wrong end of the table. I went into Plymouth with John Sheridan and helped them to avoid relegation from the Football League into the National League.'

The size of the Plymouth is something that Gary said he couldn't truly appreciate until he was a main figure at the club.

'Something I didn't realise until I went down there was just how big of a club Plymouth is and potentially could be, especially in terms of supporters. It's nothing in comparison to Sunderland, but they are a big club in their own right.'

In addition to the coaching success, Gary has worked in recruitment, getting the right deal for players and teams.

'I've just worked away at making a living, as you do. I had some success in recruitment, made one or two clubs millions of pounds by being responsible for the signing of players who were then moved on for a profit. I'm still on my journey now, I'm working for the National League, just trying to earn a living.

Gary is currently working within the National League, which covers teams at the fifth and sixth tiers of English football. His role is important in making sure teams at this level do not lose their best players for a fraction of what they are worth and, if they do leave, that they are rightly compensated.

'I'm head of player development at the National League, so basically what I've done in the last couple of years is set up a number of licensed academies within our leagues. This will compare with the EPPP system which is in the Football League.'

On top of this, two brand new divisions are in the works, adding to an exciting and vital role which is played by Gary and others within the National League set up

'We've also developed two new leagues, which is a league in the north and a league in the south and we're just building that structure to give our clubs the opportunity to develop their own players and keep hold of them.

'What happens at the minute is, I'll give an example, if you're York City and you've developed a young player who is 14 or 15, he starts playing in your youth team at 17 but then Leeds United or Middlesbrough come along and decide they quite like him. In the current state of play they can sign him for nothing, and York City would lose out.'

We're trying to get a system in place in which, at the very least, if this situation happens, that club would be compensated for losing that player.

'It's not fair. There is a system in place, the EPPP, and you know how much a player is going to cost if you sign him. There are lots of players in the National League now who are playing in the first teams and youth teams, lots of young and very talented players. It's not fair that our clubs lose them for nothing when one of the bigger clubs come along and take a liking to them.'

Gary is thoroughly enjoying what he does for the latest and next generation of footballers, about as much as he enjoyed his playing days and particularly those days spent at Roker Park.

'They were happy times for me, very happy times indeed. It's a brilliant club with brilliant supporters, I loved every minute of it, apart from at the end where it turned a little bit, it was probably time to move. Looking back, I wish I hadn't moved, but I did, and you can't turn back the clock.'

He pointed out that most of the times when he is stopped in the streets around the UK, the first thing people mention to Gary is his time at Sunderland.

'I am proud of my association with the club, I'm proud that I played that amount of games for Sunderland. When I do travel around the country and people – not very often I have to say – stop me or when they hear my name, they still associate me with my time at Sunderland, mostly.'

Like many former Sunderland players, Gary has the hopes of a possible return to the club in the future. Although he jokingly ruled out a second spell at Sunderland in one capacity in particular.

'Maybe one day there will be the opportunity for me to return to the club in some capacity, I think that's always something I would like to do if the chance came about. It wouldn't be as a player though! I'm 51 now, I'm sure people will be pleased to know.'

Gary Owers was a reliable and regular feature in Sunderland's late 1980s to early 1990s renaissance, which was needed after sinking to the third tier for the first time in their history. His commitment to the game is something that has remained with him throughout his life, and it was clear that he looks back on his playing, coaching and recruitment career with pride.

THOMAS HAUSER

Thomas Hauser was born in April 1965 in the German town of Schopfhain, located 30 miles from the border with Switzerland. After initially starting out with his home-town club, who he played for until finishing school, Thomas moved across the border to FC Basle. His father also played football professionally for the Swiss club.

Between 1982 and 1988, Thomas scored over 30 goals for Basle in a successful period. During this time, he scored in the semi-final of the Uhren Cup, an international pre-season friendly tournament held in Switzerland, as Basle won the tournament in 1983. Thomas's goal came against FC Grenchen.

FC Basle got into financial trouble, and at the end of the 1988-89 season they were relegated to the Nationalliga B – the second tier of the Swiss football pyramid. This is when Thomas's time at the club came to an end and he moved to rivals BSC Old Boys.

Thomas played for FC Basle's rivals for approximately six months until, in February 1989, the forward moved from continental Europe to the banks of the River Wear. He signed for a reported £200,000 and made his debut, coming off the bench to replace Marco Gabbiadini, later the same month.

He has two interesting claims to fame whilst playing for Sunderland. Firstly, he scored Sunderland's last goal of the 1980s and then the first of the 1990s. This came

from Thomas scoring the equaliser in a 2-2 draw at Roker Park against Port Vale on 30 December 1989, and only six minutes after coming off the bench against Hull City at Boothferry Park on New Year's Day 1990.

He also became the first non-English player to represent Sunderland at Wembley when he came off the bench in the 1992 FA Cup Final against Liverpool.

After three years on Wearside, Thomas moved back over to Europe. He played one season with Dutch side SC Cambuur in the city of Leeuwarden. He retired after this period, making two appearances in the Netherlands.

When asked about why he wanted to play for Sunderland and how the move to

England came about after his period with FC Basle, Thomas said that it was the same ambition shared by many European players at the time.

'It always was a dream of mine, like it was at the time for any professional player, to play for an English football club. When I had the chance to get a contract I took the big chance immediately.'

He added that when he was a player Sunderland were a club with little recognition outside the UK. However, Thomas felt that this has changed with the recent coverage in the Sunderland Til I Die documentary, which dropped onto Netflix for its second series in April 2020.

'Sunderland were a club which, at the time, was not very well known outside of Great Britain. I think this is because they didn't play in European Cup games. However, because of the Netflix series, people have now realised how big and traditional the club are within England.'

The move to Sunderland was Thomas's first and only move away from continental Europe. He was still young when he moved to the North East, doing so two months before his 24th birthday.

It could have been tough for the German striker, and many in his position would have struggled with the move and transition away from family and friends.

However, it was no such problem for Thomas. Giving reasons on why he felt he fit into the club and the area, Thomas named several.

'Honesty, it wasn't hard to fit in. My natural character allowed me to adapt easily, and it helped me a lot to transition into the team and the style of football in England. Also, the Mackems are very warm and friendly people which helped a lot too.'

Thomas added that his job in a city like Sunderland, which loved football and still does to this very day, helped him to be welcomed and treated well.

'Being a professional footballer in a football-crazy city like Sunderland makes a lot of things much easier than if I had another profession, than if I would have come over as, for example, an electrician. With all respect to this profession.'

Thomas noted what life and society in Sunderland was like, and how he soon realised how much the football club meant to the people of the area.

'It did suit the club and the fans, a town where you could feel and see that not all people had it easy in life, and they have been hard workers.'

He went on to the recent politics of the decade, which had affected Sunderland and the wider region drastically in the years before Thomas's moved to Wearside. Some players might not have noticed, but the man from south-west Germany was not one of them.

Thomas said, 'When I was in Sunderland, I could see that it was hit through bad events such as the closing of the shipyards, the closure of the coal mines under Thatcher.'

Thomas ended his career playing in four different countries. When asked if there was a difference in atmosphere and where he enjoyed playing the most, Thomas said that the atmosphere of traditional English stadiums couldn't be beaten.

He said, 'No, it was more enjoyable in England. The atmosphere, especially Roker Park at the time, and the atmosphere in other English stadiums too, was always something you just can't forget, and it will always be in my mind.'

Supporters see their team play for only a few hours a week. The brunt of the time is spent on the training pitch, perfecting drills and tactics for the next match. This could be laborious to some players, although Thomas considered the training and the friendly tempo to be a fond memory.

'Also, the relaxed atmosphere in training, and being amongst the players was also more enjoyable for me. My best mates in football, I still have from my time in England.

'The players were also just less envious amongst each other too, fair play had a big meaning at the time, during a game and after the game.'

The tougher nature of the football in England then was a factor of his time at Sunderland that Thomas noted as a positive. Whether this is still the case now is unclear, but in Division Two in England in 1989 there were undoubtedly many places to hide. 'It was sometimes very physical during the games. That was what made it so special compared to playing on the continent.'

Thomas adjusted to the English game, and his nine goals in 54 appearances, along with the physical presence of his 6 ft 3in frame, made him a handful for opposition defenders.

As he was playing at Sunderland during a period in which the club was on the rise after a poor period during the mid-1980s, Thomas played alongside some names which have gone down in footballing folklore on Wearside.

When asked if he could pick one player out from his time at Roker Park as someone who was a stand-out figure, Thomas resigned to say he couldn't choose just one.

'It is difficult to say and just name one. We had a few of those players, like Eric Gates, Gary Bennett, Kevin Ball and Paul Bracewell to name just a few.'

Denis Smith was the man to bring him to England, and Thomas was complimentary of his old manager

Thomas said, 'He was not a big tactician or had a big tactical brain, which was at the time not as important as it is for the game now, but he was person who you had a lot of respect for. He was honest and a good motivator.

'I personally had – I can say now, with the distance off all the years passed – a good relationship with him.'

He felt that there was one player in the dressing room at Roker Park who got more attention than others, but given this player's reputation Thomas could understand why he was treated in such a way by his manager.

'Sometimes he perhaps listened a bit too much to Marco Gabbiadini at the time. But having said that, he was the big hero in our team at the time and he deserved to have this favouritism.'

Thomas played for Sunderland in two divisions. He spoke of the differences between the two, and what it meant for his game. He wanted to play more, but unfortunately an injury cut one of his seasons short on Wearside. The technicality and physicality was different between the two, according to Thomas, something that remains the case in the league structure of 2020.

'The biggest difference between Division One and Two was that you had the technically better players in Division One and it was less physical. Having said that, I didn't have many games after my Achilles tendon injury, so I was unable to build up more experience and comparison between the two.'

This era of English football was brimming with quality players, who would go on to be cult heroes at their clubs and the wider sporting world.

Sunderland had their fair share, but when asked who the best player he played against whilst in England was, he considered it to be John Barnes.

Barnes was two years into his ten-year career at Liverpool, where he would go on to score 84 goals and play over 300 matches for the Reds, winning several trophies along the way. Sunderland came up against many top-quality players during the one season in the top flight during which Thomas was a player, but England international Barnes was the pick of the bunch for the German.

During the course of a season, a player can travel thousands of miles to play at away matches, with some requiring an overnight stay. The geographical location of Sunderland means that their players often need to travel more than most. One season Thomas had as a Sunderland player required the Black Cats to make the journey to Plymouth, Portsmouth, Bournemouth and Brighton. These four totalled almost 3,000 miles.

Thomas spoke of what it was like on the road, and the experience that stood out the most when staying over in hotels across the country: 'Apart from a snoring Agboola next to me most of the times at away matches, nothing I would make public here.'

Back on more familiar territory, Thomas spoke about what it was like to play at Roker Park for the home team. It is an experience that has stayed with him ever since.

'The atmosphere was great because at Roker Park the pitch was very close to the fans. At big games it was electrifying, and the Roker roar at kick-off unforgettable.'

When talking about how his time at Sunderland came to an end, Thomas acknowledged that three factors of bad luck came together and his life was destined to move away from Wearside.

He said, 'The contract wasn't extended, and several unlucky things came together at once. First, I snapped my Achilles at the cup game against Bristol City in the season when we got promoted in to the First Division. I would say I had a good pre-season and I had hopes of many more games in the first XI, which was what the manager promised.

'The second factor was another bad cut on the Achilles tendon on the other foot, which meant many months without playing any games. Finally, the third was that Denis Smith was replaced as manager.'

Thomas's time as a footballer came to an end prematurely due to the Achilles injuries he had suffered.

'Eventually, I wore both Achilles injuries and a year later my career had ended. I was only 28 at the time.'

Although his time at Sunderland ended early due to injuries, Thomas said that he would have loved the opportunity to stay if it came about. Ultimately, though, he recognised the timing of the injuries as being crucial to his future at the club and in football.

'I was perfectly saddled at the time and loved to play for Sunderland. I would have signed another contract straight away. I am sure things would have worked out completely differently if I didn't have those bad injuries at the time.'

When asked if there was anything he would change about his time at Sunderland, Thomas took on a light-hearted response, gesturing that he may have enjoyed the pubs of Sunderland a bit too much during his stay in the North East.

Thomas said, 'I can't think about much now that I think back. Perhaps I could have gone on a few less trips to the pub during the week, haha!'

Thomas Hauser will always be thought of in high regards, with some Sunderland fans viewing him as a cult hero for the effort and physicality he showed at Roker Park.

He may have been used more as an impact player from the bench, fans coining the nickname of 'The German Sub' due to the majority of his appearances coming from the substitutes' bench, but Thomas has a deep admiration for the club – one which many players who were at Sunderland longer than him would not share.

PART 2
1991-99: MOVING TO A NEW HOME

The final decade of the 20th century began in a similar way to how the previous one finished. Sunderland were back in Division One after the controversial play-off final against Swindon Town, but the 1990-91 season ended in relegation back to Division Two. The following season would have gone down as another bleak campaign if not for a superb FA Cup run. Sunderland reached the final against Liverpool, and although it ended in a 2-0 win for the Reds it was a testament to the character of the squad that Denis Smith put together and Malcolm Crosby took over halfway through the season, in December 1991.

Crosby's first full season as manager was also the first campaign of changes to the Football League pyramid. Division Two became Division One, and Division One was the Premiership. Sunderland started life in the new Division One with a 21st-place finish, narrowly avoiding relegation.

Terry Butcher took over as manager in the January of this season, but he was no longer in the role by November 1993. Mick Buxton helped to guide Sunderland to a 12th-place finish; however, he couldn't stop Sunderland from once again struggling in the 1994/95 campaign and again a bottom-five finish was achieved. Before the end of the season, however, there was another new man in the hot-seat at Roker Park. This time, for more than one season.

Peter Reid kept Sunderland up, and won the Division One title in his second season. Craig Russell top scored with 13 goals as Sunderland topped the league with 83 points. The following season was the club's first in the new Premiership, and the last at their historic home of Roker Park. After 99 years, Sunderland were moving up-river to the Stadium of Light.

Unfortunately, this last season ended in relegation. Despite picking up 40 points, a total which would be enough to keep a team up in more recent years, Sunderland bowed out of the Premiership.

The 1997-98 season was the beginning of a new dawn for Sunderland. New signing Kevin Phillips racked up 29 league goals as Sunderland danced their way to a play-off place, winning 26 matches and finishing third. However, like so often in the club's history, the season ended in heartache. After the play-off final against Charlton at Wembley finished 4-4 after extra time, Sunderland lost an agonising penalty shoot-out 7-6.

There would have been fears that the squad would suffer from a 'play-off hangover' the following season; however, no such thing took place. Sunderland picked up where they left off and went two steps further, winning the division with 105 points and losing just three of their 46 league matches.

Once again Kevin Phillips shone, but it was the rest of the squad too that would come together and adapt, making the next two seasons some of the most memorable in the club's history.

Sunderland would enter the new millennium in the top four of the Premier League, with a side capable of beating any in the land.

DON GOODMAN

Don Goodman is perhaps more well known to younger people as one of the voices of the Football League. A regular commentator with Sky Sports for close to 20 years, he has covered some of the most dramatic moments across the divisions. Before picking up the microphone, however, Don had a long and fruitful playing career.

Don began his professional career with Bradford City, moving on to West Bromwich Albion and then, in December 1991, to Roker Park. Three seasons at Sunderland saw him score 47 goals in over 120 appearances. His next destination after Sunderland was Wolverhampton Wanderers before a six-month period playing in Japan. Don's last professional club took him north of the border to Motherwell.

He spoke of how his career started out and how his first club was the ideal place to play first-team football from an early age. His first club was Bradford City, but Don said that he developed once heading down to the West Midlands.

'It was ambition. I was born in Leeds; my first club was Bradford. It was a wonderful place to start your career because as a 17/18-year-old I was given a chance in the first team. I left there for West Bromwich Albion, who were a big club, newly relegated out of the top division, and that's where I developed really.

'Unfortunately, it didn't go well for the team. I scored a lot of goals for a team for which things didn't go to plan. It was about aspiring and trying to get the right team which would be the vehicle to get me to the top of the table and I felt that team was Sunderland. I'd been to Roker Park as an away player a few times and I'd always left thinking, "Crikey what would it be like to have those supporters behind you?" the Roker roar and all that. They are passionate fans.'

The answer to Don's question would come soon enough when the time for him to leave the Hawthorns arose. It was a simple decision for him, and one which would see him move to Roker Park for a considerable price in 1991.

'Once the opportunity came to leave West Brom, who had by then been relegated to the third tier, it was a no brainer for me. Denis Smith easily sold me the idea, the club, the ambition, they paid a lot for me so I liked their ambition, it was all about that really.'

It can sometimes be difficult for a player to come straight into a new team during a season, but Don concluded that his personality helped him to fit in at Sunderland quickly.

'I felt like I'd been welcomed into the group instantly. I was quite an outgoing lad anyway, but you earn your team-mates' respect by how you handle yourself, how you apply yourself in training.

Don said that he found instant friendship with two players who were also new signings for Sunderland at roughly the same time.

'There were a couple of other new signings in John Byrne and Anton Rogan, I was staying in the County Hotel with them anyway, so I became close with them and I remain so to this day. The settling in period was very easy, they were a great bunch of lads who were very welcoming.

'I joined in the December, it was a club that was probably in the middle of the table but needed a good second half to the season and maybe make a push for a play-off spot. You could feel that the lads felt they could do better, maybe a tiny sense of underachieving.

But the season wasn't over, there was a lot to play for. Then of course the FA Cup started, and we all know what happened with that, so there was optimism.'

Don felt that the atmosphere in the dressing room and in his everyday experiences at the club was one of optimism. He could sense that the players knew they could improve going into the new year.

'I would say it was pretty positive. When you say see eye to eye, I mean in those days players were naturally vocal, would naturally call each other out, would naturally encourage each other. Sometimes you had to accept criticism, so from that perspective that would go on at every single club. It's not like now where, with respect, players are more sensitive.'

Don admitted that the players in the dressing room during his time at Sunderland were better at handling the criticism than footballers in the present day.

'Not many modern-day footballers respond well to a roasting or any harsh criticism. But that was the norm back then. We had leaders in the dressing room, Tony Norman in goal and obviously Bally, Gary Owers, Gordon Armstrong. Everyone was vocal and everyone was a leader. When it was time to have a few choice words with each other, it was done. It was never taken in bad spirit. It was always taken in the same knowledge that everyone wanted what was best for the team. '

About supporters, Don said that Sunderland fans weren't the first to fully get behind him and he said that he gave his all whilst at the club.

'Don't get me wrong, West Brom supporters were the first to put me on a pedestal, for want of a better expression, and chant my name, making me feel ten feet tall. I think the Sunderland fans took to me very quickly.

'They would get maximum effort and a desire to win from me. I wanted to do the best I could for them, my team and myself. That's all fans want. Even now, if fans see you giving your all, but it's not quite happening for you, they'll give you that. They see players almost throwing in the towel.'

He has fond memories of how Sunderland fans treated him on his debut and, despite the last-minute defeat, were behind their team all afternoon.

'They took to me very well, obviously the first game was a nightmare at Wolves, stepping off the coach as an ex-West Brom player I got lots of abuse. We also ended up being down to nine men at Molineux and ended up losing in the 89th minute to a wonder goal.

'That wasn't the greatest start, but I remember they travelled in their thousands on that day and after five minutes the game was up basically. They sang and chanted for the lads throughout. I knew instantly how good the Sunderland fans were.'

This admiration for Sunderland supporters has followed Don through into his broadcasting career and every time he covers a match involving the club.

'Even now as a commentator for Sky, going to Sunderland matches and seeing the enormous following, it still warms my heart to be honest with you.'

Don played for many managers during his career and struggled to identify many he didn't see eye to eye with. At Sunderland, neither manager he played under was frowned upon by Don.

'I got on well with every manager I played for, in the main, there was probably one or two who I didn't quite get on with elsewhere. Yet at Sunderland I got on with all the managers I played under.

'I had a lot to thank Denis Smith for, taking me to the club and paying what was a lot of money back then, and showing faith in me that I could be the man to score the goals. Marco Gabbiadini had not long left when I joined, and there wasn't long left of the season, so it was another show of faith.

Don was at the club less than a month before he saw the man who signed him depart. His replacement was someone whose niceness Don felt held him back as a manager in the game.

'I got on fantastic with Denis; unfortunately, his tenure wasn't a long one when I was there. It was only a few weeks. Then it was Crozza [Malcolm Crosby] and if you ask anyone who has met him, they'll say he's one of the nicest men you can meet.

'Ultimately as a number one, that's maybe something which would hold him back. I think he was the perfect number two, the perfect coach, but maybe the nice edge held him back as a manager. You never really saw a nasty edge and even now in modern football there needs to be that edge. I don't think he ever had that, but I don't think there's anyone he couldn't get on with.'

Don was brought to Sunderland to fill the goalscoring void left by Marco Gabbiadini, who left the club for Crystal Palace. Marco scored 74 times in over 150 appearances for Sunderland, but Don said that he wasn't concerned about any pressure placed on his shoulders.

'I didn't give it a second thought, same as with the transfer fee. For me it was about having confidence in my ability to score goals, which at that phase in my career I was doing. There was no reason why that wouldn't continue after I arrived at Sunderland.

'I was able to get off the mark in my second game and went on to score a reasonable amount of goals for the club. I didn't really think of who I was replacing or how much money I was signed for.'

Don moved to Sunderland because of the optimism he felt the club had to get into the First Division, but three years down the line he saw that in order to play in the top tier he would need to move on once again.

When asked about his departure from Sunderland, Don said, 'I felt that we had laboured. I was at Sunderland for exactly three years and hadn't really got close to promotion to the Premier League or a shot at the play-offs and at that time Wolves were the ambitious club of the division under Sir Jack Hayward. He was allowing manager Graham Taylor to bring in some high-quality players.

'I just felt it was almost a certainty that I would get promoted to the top division with Wolverhampton Wanderers. Unfortunately, it didn't quite happen. We were in the play-offs twice and lost on both occasions, but with the quality we had at Wolves we shouldn't have even been in the play-offs, but that's another story.'

It was a tough decision, but Don chose to leave Wearside to further his own career, one which passes quickly according to the Yorkshireman.

'That was the motive for me to leave, that I didn't really see where Sunderland were heading other than mid-table in the Championship. A football career goes by very quickly, you need to look at yourself. When the opportunity came to move to Wolves, it was one I couldn't pass up.

If it was possible to see into the future, then Don said he, of course, would have remained at Sunderland. He would undoubtedly have been a vital member of Peter Reid's squad.

"I couldn't envisage what would happen at Sunderland over the next four to five years, if I had a crystal ball it might have been different.

'You make what you think is the best decision at that time; my reason for leaving Sunderland was ambition to play at the highest level.'

When time was up on his career at Wolverhampton Wanderers, Don was given the opportunity to travel overseas and play in a very different setting to that of the West Midlands or the north east of England. In 1998 Don signed for Sanfrecce Hiroshima in the south of Japan. Talking about his experience in Asia, he talked of how the move came about and why it was something he wanted to do.

'I went from Sunderland to Wolves, stayed there for four years and tried to get to the Premier League.

'My contract was up and at the time I was playing under one of the managers I didn't get on with too well. Despite scoring a good amount of goals, I wasn't offered a new deal. I then got the chance to go on a new adventure in a new country and culture. I won't lie, the money was tempting as well. When you throw these things together, especially from a lifestyle perspective, it was a no-brainer really.'

Don said that he had grabbed the attention of the Japanese club by scoring in a televised FA Cup tie. When Hiroshima found out that he was out of contract, the enquiries soon began.

'I had scored the winner in the quarter-final of the FA Cup against Leeds United at Elland Road to take Wolves into the semi-finals. The club had seen that performance, it was broadcast in Japan, and when they found out my contract was up they made tentative enquiries to see if I would be interested.

'That's how it all came about really, they were being managed by Eddie Thomas, who is a Scottish manager, and a couple of backroom staff who were also British.'

For Don, it was a part of his career and life that he had no regrets about. He found it to be an amazing place to both live and work.

'They invited me over, and once I had a look around the facilities, places to live, schools for the kids, it all fit into place really. It was one of those periods in my life where I look back with great fondness.

'I have no regrets at all about going to Japan, and the standard of football was surprisingly higher than I had perhaps anticipated as well. Although it was a short, six-month stay, it was a fantastic life experience and something I won't forget.'

As mentioned, Don is one of the most recognisable voices in live football coverage. When asked if he ever considered taking up coaching, he gave a damning but reasonable answer as to why it wasn't for him.

'I very quickly decided that I didn't want to do the coaching thing, basically because of the sacking culture which was creeping into football. I felt that I would probably need to take a job further down the leagues. Often when this happens, you're trying to manage and coach a club with one hand tied behind your back in terms of promises made about resources. Then there is that fear that if things don't go well in the first four, five, six months you end up getting sacked from your first job.

'The pressure and the strain with what is a 24-hour-a-day job in which it's a struggle to switch off made me realise that there were better opportunities for me elsewhere.'

Before entering the media, Don created a fitness group which unfortunately, after funding was ceased, needed to be closed down.

'I went back to school and got some qualifications in personal training and nutrition and set up a health and fitness business which transformed into a health and fitness education centre. I did that up until about five years ago. We relied on college funding. Once the funding dried up and things got cut it was time to wrap that up.'

It was bits and pieces of media work that Don did as well as running the group which gave him the taste and experience to do more.

'Alongside that I was doing local media, summarising the sport on local radio. I ended up on Radio Five Live before Sky approached me about doing some games for them. This is now my 14th season [2019-20] covering games. It's a role and a job which I absolutely love. I'm on my way to Leicester as we speak.

Don spoke in more detail about the role which many football fans have come to know him in. He said that the job he does is a dream.

'I absolutely love the diversity of it. I predominantly cover the Championship; I love doing that. I'll sometimes do a Premier League game if I haven't got a Football League match to cover. Going around the country to different grounds and watching the different levels of football, it's refreshing and thoroughly enjoyable.

Going to a different ground each week has given Don the chance to see the love which supporters have every time they follow their team. We spoke in the week following the removal of Bury FC from the Football League, a week that was a miserable one for English football.

'It pleases me to see the passion every football fan has for their club. You turn up at the ground and see how much the team means to the fans, that's why it has been such a desperately sad week for football in terms of what has happened with Bury and what's gone on there.

'That is now my job, it gives me an opportunity to enjoy a reasonable amount of free time, play a bit of golf, get to the gym and socialise. I'm thoroughly enjoying it.'

Don had talked often about his admiration for Sunderland fans, and this has carried on throughout his life, most recently, at the 2019 League One play-off final when the Black Cats suffered a last minute 2-1 defeat to Charlton Athletic at Wembley Stadium. Don was on Sky Sports duties that day and, despite the heart break for Sunderland, he received warm greetings from supporters in and around the ground.

'I covered the play-off final at Wembley, and obviously it didn't end well for Sunderland, and even after that I was walking up the hill towards the hotel where I was staying and the amount of love and respect Sunderland fans still had for me really blew me away.

'It reminded me of the good days. I had three remarkable years at the club and the best thing about it was the affiliation I had with the supporters.

'I spoke about the West Brom fans putting me on a pedestal, the Sunderland fans did the same. They made me feel ten foot tall, sang my name every week, and made it three of the best years I've had as a player to be honest.

Don Goodman loved the Sunderland supporters and, overall, the supporters returned the favour. He had an impressive track record of scoring goals throughout his career, and at Roker Park this was no exception.

He wanted to show his gratitude to Sunderland supporters, concluding the interview with a special line for Black Cats fans.

'If there is an opportunity here for me to thank the Sunderland fans for the support they gave me, I would like to take it.'

Don will be remembered more for his time as a familiar face and voice in the media by many football fans, but a certain generation of Sunderland supporters will always look back with fondness on his time at the club and the work rate he always produced when wearing a Sunderland shirt.

PAUL STEWART

Paul Stewart, unlike many of the players included in this book, made his breakthrough and himself a household name before moving to Wearside. The striker made his professional breakthrough with Blackpool. Signing as a professional in 1981, Stewart would go on to score 50 goals in over 200 appearances for the Tangerines. Form like this attracted the attention of Manchester City, who Paul signed in 1987.

Another impressive goals-to-appearance tally, over 25 in just over 50 matches, turned even more heads across the top division of English football, and in 1988 Paul had earned himself a move to Tottenham Hotspur. He once again shone at White Hart Lane, making three appearances for England and winning the FA Cup during his spell in the capital. Paul scored the first in a 2-1 win over Nottingham Forest at Wembley Stadium in the 1991 final.

The summer of 1992 saw Paul sign for Liverpool for a sum of £2.3 million, a relatively large amount at the time. However, he struggled at Anfield, and during his four-year spell he was loaned out to several clubs, the last of which was Sunderland.

Although the initial loan spell would end abruptly, Paul returned to Roker Park in March 1996. Paul spent 15 months at Sunderland, scoring five times in 34 appearances and helping the club to the Division One title at the end of the 1996 season.

With hopes of moving closer to his family home in Blackpool, Paul put pen to paper at Stoke City in June 1997, scoring three times at the Britannia Stadium before his final move in 1998 to Workington.

Going back to his first move to Sunderland, Paul spoke of how it came about and why his time at Liverpool had failed to truly materialise.

'I was not having the best time at Liverpool if I'm being brutally honest, things hadn't worked out for many different reasons. I don't want to make excuses for that, but it just wasn't happening.

'Peter Reid contacted me and got me in on loan initially. I joined and played a reserve game. I went in for a challenge and did in my knee ligaments. It sort of ended there almost as soon as it began. I was obviously disappointed because I saw it as another opportunity to really get my career back on track, but I was out for a good six to eight weeks. However, Peter came back in for me later to sign me on loan again. I grabbed the chance with both hands.

'The club needed a striker, they needed someone with experience. They were flying high in the old Second Division, they just wanted somebody with a bit of experience to play upfront with Craig Russell and to help the younger lads along. Peter saw me as the ideal candidate for that.'

Paul's gratitude to Sunderland and to the manager at the time, Peter Reid, shone throughout the conversation, and he made it abundantly clear from the off. He said that the move to Roker Park was a way to rejuvenate his career.

'So that's how I ended up at Sunderland. I have got to be honest, I owe Peter Reid and Sunderland an awful lot. My career was going down the pan, I was struggling with my mental health, I was doing things off the pitch which I shouldn't have been doing, and it helped me to get refocused again and help a really good side. We won the championship and went up into the Premier League.

The first spell at Sunderland ended in frustration for Paul as he was back at Liverpool in the treatment room very soon after his debut, but Peter Reid kept in touch with him during the recuperation period.

'To honest with you, he kept in touch with me to see how I was from the injury. I always knew he was still interested in me perhaps coming back at some point, but you just never know. Ligament injuries can be career threatening; at the time I wasn't sure where it would take me.

'Thankfully I was able to get fit and get back to Sunderland. Like I said, I was joining a really good side, so it was quite easy to fit in. They had a lot of good young players and they just needed that experience around them.'

Paul noted that he was signed by Reid to bolster Sunderland's attack and to be the final piece of the attacking jigsaw. When asked if he felt this put him under any pressure, the man from Manchester replied, 'Not really, to be honest. I had known Reidy over many years, having played against him, and knowing him as an individual. He was instrumental in giving me the confidence by saying, "Look, we know what you can do, as long as you can keep your head in the right place, we believe you will do it for us. Just do what you can and what we know you can and we're sure that you'll do well here."'

The relief and appreciation of being able to get regular first-team football which he enjoyed was a lot for Paul. He felt he had something to prove at Sunderland after a poor spell in his career. The amount of money Liverpool paid for him was something that was on Paul's mind.

'That's what happened during that title-winning season. I enjoyed playing first-team football again, there were some fantastic players around me. It was like my career was revitalised, I wasn't nervous, and I wasn't anxious or anything. I just wanted to go and prove I was a good player despite what had happened at Liverpool, which was that I didn't succeed there after going for an awful lot of money.

Paul noted that he soon came to love the passion and enthusiasm from the people at Sunderland, both on and off the pitch.

'I think every town has an infinity with the fans, and it can be totally different from one town to the next. What I realised was that the fans at Sunderland were really passionate about the club, the players who were at the club, especially the ones from the North East, were passionate about the club. I bought into all that.

He added that the spirit and attitude of Peter Reid epitomised what the club was all about during this period.

'I knew Reidy was a passionate man and manager. If you gave him 100 per cent, he would always stand by you. It was one of those things really, it's what the club were all about. I loved that it was like that, the passion of the place. From the players but even more so the fans.'

It was established early in the conversation that Paul had, and still has, a lot of admiration for the man he thanks for helping to reignite his footballing career. Paul said that the players at the club would have been there because they wanted to play for their manager, and he was no different.

'I still speak to Peter, I spoke to him last Friday, I keep in touch. He wasn't just my manager he became a good friend. I always liked him as a player. I always knew he was driven, that and his enthusiasm were fantastic. He had a buzz about him, and it made you want to do well for him. That wasn't just me, I think that would have been anyone who came across him or played for him.'

The no-nonsense honesty Reid had within his style as a character and a manager is a factor Paul believes made him popular and a success, especially at Sunderland.

'He was black and white. There were no grey areas with Reidy. If you weren't doing it then he would let you know about it. But also, if you were doing it, he would let you know that you were doing a good job for him.'

After an uncomfortable few years, it was clear that Paul had rediscovered himself at Sunderland, adding that he thoroughly enjoyed his time at the club because of the honest way Reid came across to his players.

'You can't ask any more from a manager than the honesty which Peter Reid gave you. I couldn't say that about every manager I played under, but I could with him. He had honesty in abundance and was honest as the day is long. I flourished under him in that first season.'

Moving on to his team-mates, Paul said that there was a mix of youth and experience, naming players in both categories who brought a lot to the team. He fit into the latter, bringing with him well over 400 league appearances and 100 goals to Roker Park. '

'There were some really good young players in the squad. They had experience, in Paul Bracewell and Kevin Ball, but when you look at Micky Gray, Michael Bridges, Richard Ord, they were good players in a team which I think I complemented.'

Paul said his being complementary came in the form of being a link-up player for fellow forward Craig Russell.

'I was sort of the missing link up front for Craig, he needed someone to get hold of the ball. I was that missing player who Reidy needed.'

Sunderland, like most football clubs in the English game, have never been lucky enough to have an endless pot of money to spend on new players.

Paul admitted that the move was beneficial to himself and the club, due to the loan option being available, meaning Sunderland didn't need to spend lots of money to get the kind of player they needed.

'They didn't have the money to go splashing out on an expensive striker at that time, so to get me on loan probably helped them. Like I said, it worked for both parties.'

Paul played a significant part in a special yet poignant match in Sunderland's history. He scored one of the club's final goals at their old home, Roker Park. Sunderland beat Everton 3-0; however, their last season at the ground which they called home for 99 years would end in relegation from the Premier League.

Our conversation took place in the days following the 23rd anniversary of the match, and Paul said that one of his former team-mates got in touch. The pair reminisced about this match and their time together at Sunderland.

'I saw a lot of things on Twitter about that, that's why I'm laughing. Micky Gray contacted me, and we were talking about the good old days.'

Paul talked through the emotions of playing that game, and how the main priority for the players was to get the points. The players didn't let the emotion of the day get to them. He scored a penalty that day, and he was determined to get the job done from the spot.

'It was momentous in the fact that it was the last game at Roker Park, which was an iconic ground to say the least. When the penalty was awarded, I didn't really think twice about it. We needed a win anyway because we were struggling that season, there's no doubt about it. All things being equal, I wanted to stand up there.'

Taking a penalty wasn't something Paul was used to that season, but he jumped at the opportunity to take one that day. The significance of the game he was playing in wasn't in his mind when he stepped up to the mark.

'Being one of the three players to score in the last game at the ground wasn't something that entered my head when we were awarded the penalty. I never thought about making a part of history at the club, it was really more about needing the three points. I was comfortable with taking it.

'I didn't usually take them, but we'd missed a few during the season and I just stepped up and said I would take them. Then we got one against Everton which I scored.'

Roker Park was famous across the country for its atmosphere. It was a place where opposition teams would not enjoy visiting, one of the group of classic footballing arenas in the UK; the number has since shrunk further.

Paul explained how the ground's famous atmosphere played its part during this final match, but added that the day was tinged with sadness with everyone realising that the final whistle would bring about more than just the end of the match that afternoon.

'The atmosphere was electric, absolutely electric. The passion of the fans and the way they were made it a very special day. It was also a sad day in some respects, in that one of the most iconic grounds in the country was going to come to an end.

'There were mixed feelings with the players in terms of Roker Park being one of the iconic grounds you went and played at. You knew when you went to play there as an opponent that the atmosphere was going to be electric. That was whether it was the last game or not. It was great to have been part of a stadium like that.'

Paul's time on Wearside came to an end in the summer of 1997, but he explained that he was far from forced out of the club; a fate which many others would say befell them in the past and since Paul's time at Sunderland.

As it was, it was a case of needing to put personal commitments first, a decision which manager Peter Reid was sympathetic and understanding about, according to Paul.

'I did want to stay longer and I didn't have to leave. Arguably I didn't have my best season and we went down, the season after we went up. Peter wanted me to stay but I was living in a hotel and my wife was over in Blackpool where I lived. My children were there too.

'It was me who said to Peter if anyone comes in for me in that area, around the north-west area, would you consider me going. He understood and said yes. Stoke were the club who came in for me. Playing for them meant that I was able to travel from my own home and back without living away from my family. That was the only reason I left. Like I said, Peter did want me to stay.'

Paul hung up his boots in 2000, but in 2016 he and several other players made the incredibly brave decision to come out and talk about abuse they received as young players. It is this experience that has shaped the vital work which he now carries out.

'You'll probably be aware of what happened in 2016, when lots of players came forward to talk about abuse they received at the hands of paedophile coaches. I was probably the highest profile to come forward.

'Since then, I've been working in safeguarding. This includes giving talks to schools, colleges and universities. I also work with the EFL doing workshops at academies talking to coaches and parents. Really, my work now is on safeguarding.'

He spoke of the reaction he received after coming forward, with many people being surprised. It showed this kind of abuse can happen to anyone and people with any kind of attitude or character.

'There was no doubt that people were shocked that a player like myself, it often gets mentioned, that it would happen to someone like me. People say, "We didn't think it would happen to you Stewie of all people".'

Paul said that he hopes his work encourages people who were in his position to come forward and talk about their experience, but he added that there is a deeper issue at hand and another, greater focus.

'Hopefully it gives people the inspiration to come forward but the main focus is that it can't happen again. We want to make sure that we have all the procedures and policies in place as well as the correct reporting structure if a young footballer does have an issue. That can be any issue, whether they are being bullied or a different type of abuse. Ultimately, it's to protect people.'

Paul wants to get the message across to clubs and individuals in the sport that keeping abusers out of football is vital. His safeguarding role takes him up and down the land, and it will continue to do so.

'My main goal is to hopefully make clubs and people understand that we need to keep these individuals out of the game because, unfortunately, they are still around. If we don't put all the right measures in place, they will try and infiltrate and prey upon youngsters again.'

Going back for his final thoughts on his time at Sunderland, Paul enjoyed it immensely. His admiration for the players he played with and the fans who he played in front of was clear; he undoubtedly developed a soft spot for the club.

'I met a lot of great and passionate footballers and supporters. I like to think that I gave my all. I know it didn't quite work out in the second season, but I thoroughly and immensely enjoyed my time at Sunderland Football Club. I always look out for their results; I always hope they do well, and I hope to see them back in the big time soon.'

Paul Stewart is a player who enjoyed a blistering period as a player and came to Sunderland with a solid reputation. He suffered an injury blow in his first Sunderland debut, but returned to be an important cog in the red-and-white promotion machine. He enjoyed a fruitful career which included a goal and a win in an FA Cup Final as well as a Division One winner's medal with Sunderland.

His role in the game now is of great importance and carrying on his important work will help to make sure abusers can no longer damage young people from within the safety of the sport they love.

DARREN WILLIAMS

Born in Middlesbrough, Darren Williams started his professional career with York City. He spent two years with the Minster Men before joining Sunderland in October 1996 for a fee of £50,000. Darren was an integral part of Peter Reid's side through the late 1990s and early 2000s.

He experienced the highs of finishing seventh in the Premier League in back-to-back campaigns and the lows of an agonising penalty shoot-out defeat in the Division One play-off final. Williams went on to play 237 times across eight years on Wearside, finding the back of the net on six occasions.

Throughout his career Williams went on to play for Cardiff City, Hartlepool, Bradford and Dundee United, before finishing his career not too far from his home at Whitby Town; a club he went on to manage. It was his time at Sunderland, however, that many football fans will feel was his best.

Sat in his home in one of the many beautiful parts of County Durham, Darren regaled of his years playing at Sunderland. Hoping to kick off the chat on a nice, positive note, we spoke about the occasion of Sunderland's 2-1 win at St James' Park in November 2000.

The build-up to any North East derby is electric, but Darren recalled what it was like to be a Sunderland player arriving at St James' Park and how the high-octane spirit between teams in a derby was replaced with a far darker attitude.

'It's such a hostile place to go, when we arrived and pulled under the canopy it was just jam-packed with Newcastle fans. As we stepped off the bus, it was just a pure hatred. You get the banter between a lot of clubs, but this was a pure hatred.'

Darren acknowledged that his boss at that time perhaps got more thrown at him from the Newcastle fans than any of the players.

'To be fair it probably wasn't half as bad as what Peter Reid got, that guy took some stick, but fair play to him he took it on the shoulders. He got us into the dressing room and got his point across, how he wanted us to play the game and what he wanted to do and basically we went out and did the business for him.'

The whole experience of the Derby is surely a special one for any player lucky enough to play a part. On this occasion it was Darren's first taste of one of the fiercest rivalries in English football.

'It was a rivalry I'd never experienced before and going there and coming away with three points was amazing.'

For fans, it can often be very tense, but Darren recalled that there wasn't much tension in the dressing room. The players had a job to do, and it would be a day at the office to remember.

'There was no pressure really, we just went out there and enjoyed the match. It really sets you up for the next game. In the back of your mind you have that thought of we must win this game. If we didn't win another game that season, I'm sure the fans would only have remembered that match.'

To the neutral, a derby would just look to be a battle for three points. However, everyone associated with Sunderland knows that a win against Newcastle feels like it's worth about ten wins. Darren knew all too well the importance of claiming the win against the old enemy.

'To come away from that game with all three points was amazing.'

Darren played under many managers in his near 20-year playing career, but during our chat it quickly became apparent that one boss made a greater impact than any other: the man who brought him to Sunderland, Peter Reid.

'My relationship with him was brilliant, he's the best manager I've played with, hands down. He was a great man-manager. For him and Bobby Saxton to put together a side, on probably one of the lowest budgets in the league, which achieved two seventh-place finishes was unbelievable.

'He looked after people; he knew how to talk to people. He knew the players who needed a kick up the backside and he knew the players that need a cuddle. I got on extremely well with both him and Bobby Saxon, they were fantastic for me whilst I was at the club.' It was never the most flamboyant of coaching duos, but Reid and Saxon pieced together one of the best Sunderland sides in recent history, and Darren was a major part of this for several years.

For those on the outside looking in, it's easy to only look at football managers in a professional sense. For Darren, he got to see a side to Peter Reid which few would have seen as his manager showed a highly compassionate side during a tough personal time.

'Unfortunately, when we were at Manchester City away one season, we were staying overnight, and my dad died so I had to shoot off back home to Middlesbrough. Peter Reid stood up and threw me his car keys but straight after asked if I wanted anyone to drive me home.

'I was like, it's alright, I'll drive myself home, but you know he was there for me. I joined Sunderland as a kid, and I think he decided to take me under his wing. It's things like that which you'll never forget.'

It may seem like a simple gesture from Reid, but talking about it made it clear that it meant a great deal to Darren. When a manager puts himself out there for his team, the respect will be reciprocated.

The conversation headed back towards events on the pitch and to a time where Darren scored the winner at Middlesbrough, helping to push his home-town club closer to relegation. Looking back on the highlights, it's fair to say he made the most of his celebrations.

The goal was deserving of it, however. A beautifully flighted, in-swinging free kick from the by-line was finished off in style by Darren. He spoke of how he expected to get some comments from friends and family once he'd left the pitch at the Riverside Stadium.

'All my family are from Middlesbrough and you're half expecting some stick from mates, but they were ok about it really. At the end of the day I was there doing my job, playing football for Sunderland.'

Darren was born and bred in Middlesbrough but on numerous occasions during his recalling of his career he told of how Sunderland were a team that quickly became close to his heart. This seems to have changed little in the years following his departure from the Stadium of Light.

He said, 'I fell in love with Sunderland because the fans are so passionate. My time there was brilliant. Yeah, I was born in Middlesbrough, I grew up watching Middlesbrough as every local lad would, but when I scored the goal I reacted like a typical non-goalscorer, I was buzzing.'

His celebrations against his home-town club would have perhaps annoyed most supporters in the Riverside that day, but once some context is added it's easy to see why Darren celebrated in the manner he did.

The level of anger from Middlesbrough fans crossed a line in the days following, as Darren explained:

'I took a lot of stick from fans during the warm-up, so when I scored I thought I deserved to give them some back. After that there was a lot of abuse from fans. I had my car windows smashed, which was taking it too far, but still at the time I had no mixed feelings when I scored, I was there to do a job for Sunderland.'

Darren's professional attitude to scoring at his home-town club is something that isn't seen too much in football these days.

Unfortunately, Darren couldn't pride himself on playing in a division higher than his home-town club as, despite scoring the winner in April 1997, Sunderland were relegated from the Premiership along with Middlesbrough just weeks later.

Darren played a huge part in two of the most successful seasons of the modern era for Sunderland. Following on from a record-breaking promotion from the Championship, clocking up 105 points in the 1998/99 season, they took the Premier League by storm.

The following seasons saw Sunderland finish seventh in consecutive seasons and defeats were very few and far between. The first of these campaigns, 1999/2000, saw Kevin Phillips win his European golden boot for his 30 goals in 34 appearances – still the only Englishman to do so.

Darren loved being a part of these years, however; just to play in the top division was special and it was a chance he grabbed with both hands: 'To be involved with the club full stop was great. It was something I'd dreamed of, playing in the Premier League and playing on a big stage like that with Sunderland was great.

The isolation of players and managerial staff from fans is almost a given in 2018. Up until the takeover from Stewart Donald and Charlie Methven in June 2018, this was very much the case at Sunderland. Former owner Ellis Short was rarely even in the north east of England, never mind at the Stadium of Light, and a time for change was needed.

When Darren started at Sunderland, he marvelled at the close relationship between everyone involved at the club.

'The good thing is, which I always revert to, is that at the time I was at the club it was one. The chairman, the board, the players, the staff, the fans. We were all one. Now it feels as though there are sections all over the place. At the time I was there it felt like we were one big family.'

Sunderland fans across the world couldn't believe how well their side did in this first campaign back in the Premiership, but Darren realised that it wasn't a fluke. He was always aware that this team he played in didn't stop until the full-time whistle.

'The strong bond between the players Peter Reid had brought together deserved their success, it's just that we were so confident in each other, we were such good mates that we would die until the end of the game for each other.

'If we were 1-0 down, we all knew we weren't beaten until we left that pitch. From our point of view, we were collectively together, and we stuck together.'

This bond created a confidence which, Darren explained, led many of the side's critics to claim they were overly confident with their own abilities. He himself thought otherwise.

'We were on the crest of a wave. Even if we went a goal down, we just knew that we'd have the chance to get back into the game. People used to say it was cocky, it wasn't a cockiness and it wasn't arrogant.

The two campaigns at the start of the noughties were some of the best years Sunderland AFC have ever had, but they were also seasons that left fans wondering 'what if?', and Darren believed that the side he was part of were good enough to make the next big step and do something no Sunderland team had done since 1973. Even a single season playing European football would surely have seen thousands fly from Wearside to wherever Sunderland might have been drawn to play.

He felt that if it wasn't for a few flat performances during the season, Europe could have been a possibility.

'I think we could have gone that one step further and got into Europe. If we look at it there were probably occasions where we didn't perform particularly well, and we let ourselves down and dropped some points. We knew each other's abilities and we knew how well we could all perform, but there were some games where we didn't perform, and we didn't live up to the expectations of not just others but ourselves too. We knew what we could do.'

This tight-knit group of players deserved a chance of getting stuck into Europe – one could dare to say they'd hold their own against most of the sides they would have faced in the early rounds.

The man from Middlesbrough fulfilled a dream at Sunderland, but he wouldn't mind doing a bit more on Wearside. Darren did more than rule out a return to Sunderland, he openly hopes to re-join the club in a different capacity.

'I get back to the club as much as I can. An ambition of mine was to play in the Premier League and it's something I achieved with Sunderland. My ambition now is to get involved with the club again in some way. I want to coach there; in an ideal situation you want to manage there.

'You want to be involved because you've spent so many good years at the club and it's a massive club. It's a shame to see where it is now and has been in recent years.'

It's easy for former players to talk about how much they care about a football club; however, Darren took the opportunity to show how much Sunderland means to him by helping with some DIY back in the summer.

'I do want to be back in some capacity, I go back when I can. I went and helped with the changing of the seats. I go to the games when I can. I love to be part of the club and I want to be back involved full time.'

This doesn't sound like a man who says these things for the sake of it – because it isn't. To use a phrase lovingly uttered by Mackems everywhere, 'He loves the lads'.

Since hanging up his boots, Darren has taken a dip into the often-turbulent waters of coaching, even being given his debut as a manager at Whitby Town in Yorkshire.

'Since retiring I've been involved in some coaching. I was manager at Whitby for four years so I've kind of had a look at that side of things and I know what is required.' It seemed like a period of his career which he relished, helping to whet his managerial appetite.

He quickly discovered the difficulties of being a manager in the cut and thrust which is the depths of the footballing pyramid.

'Managing at non-league level is so tough, you can't just go out and buy players when you want. We [at Whitby] found it tough as we didn't have a great attraction.'

Darren did, however, do a great job on a shoestring budget, something which he rightly spoke of with pride. The kind of turnaround he oversaw would be impressive for a side with 100 times the money he had at his disposal; for Darren to do what he did at a Northern League side was nothing short of remarkable.

'When I took over we were 13 points adrift in October, the chairman had written us off. He said we were going into the Northern League and he was planning for it. My thought was 'give me a month', I at least wanted a chance to settle in first before he started saying 'we're going to get relegated'. I did say to him at the time that I'll prove him wrong.'

Darren did exactly that and that chairman was hopefully grateful for the job he did.

He told of how reshaping a team was a tough task, but with some help he managed to get his side sorted for their relegation fight. The first step was to make sure the players at the club had what it takes for a scrap down the wrong end of the table.

'We managed to change the team in the space of the month – myself, Dave Campbell and Dennis Wheeler. We got a few players out who unfortunately didn't meet our criteria, but I did find places for them to go. I didn't just say 'thanks very much' and let them go, I don't believe in that. it's important to look after players who want to carry on their career.'

This caring attitude even to players leaving the club shows that Darren has the compassionate side often required by the best managers. It would soon be apparent who he'd learnt this from during his playing career.

Taking over with his side so far adrift at the foot of the table was going to be a tough task for any manager, never mind one who was embarking on his first job. Nevertheless, Darren and his managerial team proved their chairman wrong.

'We turned it around and we went on a 16-game unbeaten run at the back end of the season, which kept us up. The season after that we finished 11th on one of the smallest budgets in the league. Season after, we came ninth so there was progression but unfortunately the chairman started to pull the money out, which was the killer.'

This caused Darren to leave his role, but despite it ending in these circumstances he could still come away from Whitby knowing he'd done a fantastic job with very little resources.

The period as a manager tested Darren, making him go to some length to get his part-time players on board. This was achieved, partially through his ability to keep spirits up, which is something he seems to excel in.

'It was a great experience; I was having to get lads out of work on building sites and down to Nantwich for midweek games and they were coming back up late at night to start work the next morning again.

'The motivation side of it was very difficult but we managed it.'

It was here he admitted he'd been able to put into action what a certain Sunderland manager taught him. Football clubs can be successful without having an open chequebook at hand. Sunderland were during Darren's time at the club, and in turn Darren achieved success at Whitby Town.

'I experienced more of what I learnt at Sunderland under Reidy. You don't have to go out and buy the most expensive players, you can buy pieces of a jigsaw and when they're together on the pitch they gel together.'

The influence of the managerial team that brought him to Sunderland has stayed with Darren throughout his career. For idols to represent in his own managerial career, Darren couldn't have done much better than his management team at Sunderland.

'I would reflect most on Peter Reid and Bobby Saxon. It was old school and it was hard. Anyone who has watched Premier Passions will know that, it's very explicit. Modern-day managers are scared about upsetting people, but when you're in a managerial position why should you be? People should respect you.'

He acknowledged that he was put into an unusual position at Whitby but moving from player to manager helped him in his latter role.

'At the end of the day, I went to Whitby and I was playing initially so I ended up telling my mates what to do. That helped though, it gave them a respect for me, and I appreciate that. It's something I'd reciprocate. Knowing how to treat your players is a big part of football.'

Darren had many team-mates during his time at Sunderland, almost all of whom were pieces of the jigsaw put together by Peter Reid and chairman Bob Murray.

Three players in particular stood out to Darren, with two being the dictionary definition of a Sunderland AFC cult hero.

'Niall Quinn was fantastic, everyone loved Quinny. I came in as a young lad and he was there as a figure to talk to. Kevin Ball, too, he'd take you under his wing but also give you the tougher side if needed. He wouldn't be shy enough to kick you in the shins in training. This was good though as if you were a young lad and he saw you getting a bit carried away he'd ground you.'

A third and perhaps lesser-known player who made an impact on Darren's time at Sunderland was American midfielder Claudio Reyna. Born in Livingston, New Jersey, Claudio was a midfielder who played almost 30 games on Wearside. He represented his country on an impressive 112 occasions, finding the back of the net eight times.

Talking of Claudio, Darren said, 'He was a player with great ability, and he was such a nice genuine lad. He knew how good he was, but he would never show it. He was a gentleman and, undoubtedly, he was an idol for many kids.'

These sorts of idols feel fewer and further between in more recent years.

Keeping players grounded is something Darren has seen throughout his playing career, right from the very start. Even before Kevin Ball, he was getting his feet kept firmly on the ground by a man who would become a regular fixture in the Sunderland coaching set up. Ricky Sbragia was a coach for many years at the Stadium of Light in the 2000s, and for most of the 2008-09 season he was sat in the hot seat.

Darren was at the mercy of Sbragia from early in his career but was grateful for the harsh lessons he was taught by the Scotsman.

'It's a massive thing, Ricky Sbragia did this for me at York when I was starting out. He kept me grounded by giving me all the worst jobs. It did its job though.'

Darren concluded by talking of how much he appreciated the Sunderland fans and the way they reacted to what they saw on the pitch.

'I loved my time at Sunderland; I loved the fans they were fantastic. Whether we won, lost or drew, I'd still applaud them at the end of the game.

'Even if I was taking stick you just must get on with it and take the rough with the smooth. We can't moan on that the fans are booing us when they have the right to do so. We'll be out there when they are singing our praises, so we must take the negatives.

'I really appreciated my time there and my ambition is to be back there in some way, shape or form.'

He won't be the only former Sunderland player to think this way, but there will be few who said it with more passion.

Darren Williams is a man who loved his spell at Sunderland and, considering how many times he played, the club loved him back.

From winning promotion back to the Premier League, to finishing seventh and winning a Tyne Wear derby at the home of Sunderland's oldest enemy, Darren was a key part of these high points and everything in between.

His old-fashioned style of defending made sure that he became a crucial part of one of the most successful Sunderland teams in modern history.

If he gets linked to becoming a coach/manager at your club in the future, you'll be getting a man who can pass on heaps of experience to your club and your players.

NICKY SUMMERBEE

Nicky Summerbee began his professional career at Swindon Town, becoming a regular performer and helping the Robins to the Premier League. After making over 100 appearances for Swindon, Nicky moved back closer to his home town of Altrincham and to Manchester City, a club where he felt a pressure to be as good as his dad. Mike Summerbee was a legend at Maine Road, scoring 47 goals in over 350 matches across a ten-year period. Nicky joined Manchester City in 1994, playing 130 matches.

A successful period at Sunderland ended when Nicky joined Bolton in 2001. Over the next five years he would ply his trade at Nottingham Forest, Leicester City, Bradford City, Tranmere Rovers and finally Tamworth in 2006.

Nicky spoke of how he was in an unusual position at Manchester City, and it was a period which he admitted didn't go to plan.

'I was at Manchester City, where it was a difficult scenario, my dad played there and was a bit of a legend at the club. Being a Manchester lad, I went to City when I found out they were interested. Unfortunately, I had a bit of a tough time and it didn't really work out.'

He was one of the select few players to appear in the first league match at Sunderland's new stadium. Nicky's appearance for Manchester City would be one of his last and his impression of the club saw him secure a move soon after.

'We went and played, I think it was the opening game where Manchester City played at the Stadium of Light, and I thought, "I would love to come here, it's fantastic". Somehow or other it must have leaked through. Next thing I knew I was getting a phone call saying that they wanted to do a swap deal, me for Craig Russell.

'It was, for me, not knowing exactly how big the club and the fan base are. It was a new challenge and one where I needed to get away from being as good as my dad. It was a difficult scenario. It was a no brainer to move to Sunderland.'

Nicky could see instantly that the dressing room at the Stadium of Light was one which he would enjoy being a part of.

'It was a fantastic dressing room, I noticed straight away. There was great camaraderie, and the place was on the up. And rightly so; the club had just moved into a brand-new stadium, started off well and straight away I realised the team spirit.

'That went on to the success of what we achieved. We did well because we had great team spirit. There were some great characters in the dressing room, your Alex Raes, Chris Makins, Lee Clarkes. all the guys there. That's what I noticed instantly; it was a breath of fresh air.'

Nicky appreciated the atmosphere in the dressing room so much that he compared it to a more recent, far less successful Sunderland squad.

'The team spirit built whilst I was there too. Sometimes you go into a situation and it works, sometimes it doesn't. I've watched the documentary on Netflix and that was a rotten dressing room, something wasn't right there.

'I don't care which manager came in, Chris Coleman or whatever, that dressing room wasn't right. It's very difficult, the best managers in the world couldn't have changed it.

'Our dressing room was completely opposite. Everyone worked hard for each other. I never came across a captain like Bally [Kevin Ball], he was the best captain I ever came across. He was organised yet fair, and you wouldn't get on the wrong side of him. We had a real mixture of everything in that dressing room, and it felt good.'

Nicky felt that he enjoyed being at Sunderland because he was perfectly cut out to play in the side that Peter Reid wanted to put together. He added that having such clinical strikers ahead of him was rewarding.

'I was very proud. To go to a massive club. I knew who I was, I could cross a ball. When I had Niall Quinn and Kevin Phillips in the box and the style we played at the time, it suited me down to the ground. To be a part of that was great.'

The period in which Nicky played at the Stadium of Light was one in which opposition teams were made to feel intimidated. He said that this, along with other thoughts of his time at the club, didn't cross his mind until after the moment has passed.

'You don't think about it. When you're in it, you don't think about it. It's when you look back and think "that was really enjoyable". Teams would come up and find it hard because of the way we played, we worked hard and got the ball back quickly.

'When we got it back, we would open up the game and get balls into the box. It was exciting and the crowd were loving it. When you get the crowd going at that place, it's a difficult place to play. everything went right for us.'

The winning feeling at the club was not just reserved for the first team either, as Nicky explained:

'At that point I think even the youth and reserve teams were both top of their leagues too. Things couldn't have gone any better through the club then.'

Nicky explained how his job was made easier by the players he had as team-mates. The squad that Reid assembled was brimming with talent; Nicky said that even if a cross he put into the box was overhit there was a good chance the attack would continue.

'With me, I didn't really need to beat a player. You had Allan Johnstone on the other side who had trickery. I knew that I could open the body up a little bit and get it into the box. If I overhit, the chances are it would find Niall Quinn, if it was front post then Kevin Phillips would be there. Everyone knew straight away what was happening.

'If I got the ball, I was getting it into the box as soon as possible. If it didn't work out, everyone worked hard to get behind the ball and win it back.' It seemed as though there was never concern that the side would be hit on the counter-attack, because of the high work rate each player had.

It suited me; it played to my strengths. I didn't need to do any defending because I had the likes of Darren Holloway and Chris Makin behind me. They did that, so when the ball came to me, I just needed to get a bit of space and then deliver the ball.

Within the period that Nicky was a Sunderland player, he appeared in some of the most memorable matches in the club's recent history. The first match that Nicky picked out as most memorable was one that saw Sunderland head up the road and turn over the old enemy in their own back yard.

To say it was a wet night on Tyneside would be an understatement. In conditions which in more recent times would probably get called off, Kieron Dyer put Newcastle

1-0 up just before the half-hour mark. This was before Niall Quinn scored a glancing header and Kevin Phillips curled home the winner 15 minutes from time. Cue chaos on Wearside and misery by the Tyne.

Nicky recalled the match with great joy, saying he loved having the opportunity to play in one of the most hostile derby matches in England.

'The game against Newcastle on the rainy night at St James' Park. We used to go out and see the Newcastle players and want to beat them. I knew of the hatred between the two sets of fans and I wanted to experience that. I would pick that performance for the things that happened, Shearer being left on the bench, going a goal behind and giving a top performance. There was a real buzz after that. We saw what it meant to all the Sunderland fans.

'Everything worked so hard together. You couldn't buy the kind of chemistry which we had at the time. We played for each other, that goes into the dressing room too.'

Nicky acknowledged the play-off semi-final in his first season at the club as a highlight. In a match where Sunderland trailed after the first leg against Sheffield United, they needed to win and had a packed Stadium of Light behind them.

'I would also say the Sheffield United play-off game for atmosphere, that takes some beating. We were trailing after the first leg. My dad was sat next to Graeme Souness at that one and they'd never experienced an atmosphere like it.'

A thumping home win against a star-studded Chelsea side was the third of Nicky's best games he has been involved in. The victory in December 1999 put Sunderland up to third in the Premier League, further adding to the hope of many a supporter that their club could achieve European football.

'The other one would be the 4-1 against Chelsea. I played on the opening game of the season when we got battered 5-0, but to put that behind us in the home game was great. We blew them away, there were some very big names in that side for Chelsea.'

Nicky said that his time at Sunderland was the best of his career. He felt that Sunderland were the only club where he was able to play his natural game, and the only club where he felt truly appreciated.

'Playing at Sunderland was the top point in my career. It was good at the start, I made it into the Premier League with Swindon Town, but it was nothing like playing for Sunderland and at a club where everyone understood what I was all about. It took a bit of time for people to understand what I was like.

'I wore long shorts, looked a bit scruffy, a bit lazy and uninterested. It wasn't a case of that though. To the eye, I would look a bit disinterested, but Sunderland fans got the chance to see what I was about.'

Nicky said that he could feel the belief that the crowd at the Stadium of Light had in him, adding that his career after Sunderland was disappointing.

'When you have that at a club, to go out onto a football pitch and know that the crowd believe in you, I've never felt more confident. I finished at Sunderland and my career was a disaster after that. I was just a journeyman; I couldn't get back to any sort of standard. I felt I shouldn't have gone; I was never offered another contract. I thought I was going to push on but unfortunately it wasn't the case.'

It was a far shorter period at the club than Nicky had hoped for, but that doesn't stop him from truly appreciating the three years he had on Wearside. He added that a lot of people underestimate the size of the club, something that Nicky realised during his time playing:

'Despite that, I still have great memories. Going out onto that pitch with 40,000 people behind you and understanding you, I never had that again. It was a highlight to be at that football club. I don't think people understand the size of Sunderland or understand what they're all about.'

We spoke just hours after Sunderland lost 1-0 to Wycombe Wanderers, and Nicky acknowledged this defeat and the Sunderland Till I Die documentary on Netflix, which has since aired its second series. He was grateful that he was able to have a better time at the club than most players and managers since the turn of the millennium.

'I watched the show on Netflix, and it was such a shame which happened. Hopefully the club get back to where they belong soon. It is a huge club. If you get it right there, it's something special. I was fortunate enough to get it right there.'

The financial situation of Sunderland has been a hot topic over the last few years, and Nicky was more than happy to throw his two pence into the matter. He used an example from one of his other former sides and expressed how Sunderland deserve better.

'If there are people looking to buy a football club and genuinely put money into the club, you look at Sunderland and where they are now. You have the fan base, it's a case of turning it around. If you do turn it around, it can easily pick up again. There's no reason why it shouldn't do that.

'Look at Manchester City for one example of how things were turned around. It's the same situation, they were in the same division. People are looking to buy clubs; the Premier League is huge now. Sunderland are in a good position in that sense.'

On Sunderland fans and the people of the wider area, Nicky said that they are passionate and ask simple things of footballers who play for their club.

'I talk to a lot of people. That part of the world is unique. They know more about football than possibly anywhere else in the world. All they want is to see the things which should be given. If you try and looking like you're working, trying to do things then the crowds will come. They will appreciate it.

'If they don't, then it's easy to see. If you do the basics right and get it going, it can really go in Sunderland's favour. That should be a given, but I get it when you're unconfident.'

He said that the style of football played by Sunderland wasn't complicated and the work rate of everyone in the side helped towards the success.

'Our football was basic; we played a 4-4-2 and we were open and expansive going forward. If we lost the ball, we all worked hard to get it back. When we did it was all about creating opportunities and getting balls into the box.'

As Nicky previously mentioned, his main job was getting the ball into the feet or head of Kevin Phillips and Niall Quinn. He admitted that having players like that in the box made this job far easier. The confidence of Nicky and his Sunderland team-mates helped towards the success of the club during this period.

'It wasn't really rocket science, stuff like that, but when you've got someone like Niall Quinn who is big it always works. You can knock a ball into Niall because of his height and then Kevin Phillips plays off him. Football is confidence. If you get the right thing going with a good group of players, it can really click.'

After leaving Wearside, Nicky said that his career never worked out. He was unable to find the heights of his time at the Stadium of Light, and it was apparent that Sunderland was the only club Nicky played at where he could sense the crowd understood him.

His look of oversized shorts and untucked shirt was one that Nicky said gave an impression of his lack of interest on the pitch. He was pleased that the Sunderland fans were able to see that this wasn't the case.

Very few players with such an ability to cross a ball have played for Sunderland. Nicky has said the strikers in front of him made his job easier, and I dare say that the strikers would feel the same way about Nicky.

As we know, footballers' retirement often leaves them with lots of spare time. Some go into coaching and others go into media coverage of the sport.

Nicky, in a way, did neither. He spoke of how he went from construction in Manchester to then setting up shop across the globe with another familiar face to Sunderland fans.

'I've been up to all sorts since retiring. I did some building in Manchester, then suddenly I got offered a job in Qatar, obviously where the World Cup is being held in 2022. Nothing was happening, I was doing some afte- dinner speaking but nothing regular, and I got offered this job.

'Believe it or not, Chris Makin came out with me and we took the chance, we absolutely love it. This is our eighth year now [in 2019] we cover the local league, work on television, and I work on both.'

Nicky is clearly enjoying what he does, which includes working with the domestic football in Qatar; a division which few outside of the country could say they are familiar with.

'Life is good, Chris loves it, we work together, and things are fantastic as we work towards the World Cup. When people find out what it's all about and see what goes into Qatar football, some of the players who are coming through, it's much better than some people think.'

He also addressed the criticism of the country that is hosting the next FIFA World Cup in 2022, saying that not enough people know about the high levels of interest in football in Qatar.

'It gets a lot of bad press, but this will be a phenomenal World Cup. We wake up and stick our shorts and flip flops on. I would like it if one day someone would send some Sunderland shorts for the beach. It's a phenomenal place, five-star living.

'We're here talking rubbish for a living now, because that's something which me and Chris are very good at.'

When asked for a final point on Sunderland AFC, Nicky took the chance to promote another of his former team-mates on Wearside.

'I would like one day for Micky Gray, who is a very good friend of mine, to be given the opportunity to coach at Sunderland. He's a Mackem lad who has a lot to offer. I would like someone to help him get to that point.

'He has a spot there, he's very passionate for the club. I don't see why not. They put a lot of names together but for me he needs to have some role at the football club. That's my last point and I really hope he gets it.'

Nicky Summerbee was the kind of winger that every manager wants to be a success at their club. His ability undoubtedly provided many goals during a golden era at Sunderland. The love for his time at Sunderland was clear throughout, as was his desire for someone to go into the club and make it work.

JODY CRADDOCK

A member of the side pieced together by Peter Reid in what was a true golden age of football at Sunderland, Jody Craddock was a lynch pin from the late 1990s through to the early 2000s. Born in Redditch, Jody made his professional debut for Cambridge United in December 1993. He was part of a clean-sheet-keeping defence, with the U's shutting out Stockport County in a 0-0 draw.

After four years plying his trade in Cambridgeshire, Jody was picked up by a talent scout from Sunderland. For £300,000 the Black Cats welcomed aboard a man who would go on to make nearly 150 appearances. However, for the first season in the Premier League on Sunderland's books he turned out for another team in red and white, making ten appearances on loan at Sheffield United in the 1999-2000 season.

His first campaign for Sunderland culminated in the penalty shoot-out defeat to Charlton Athletic in the Division One play-off final. Jody made 32 league appearances throughout the season, which ended in heartache and a missed penalty from Michael Gray.

Jody would have to wait until Sunderland's second campaign back in the Premier League to secure his place in the squad. However, he was an integral part of making sure Peter Reid's side finished seventh for the second season in a row. A solid central-defender who was good enough to keep a number of reliable defenders out of the side.

He was an ever-present for the next few years on Wearside before departing for a side closer to his home. Obviously being a man who enjoyed putting roots down within a football club, Jody followed his six years in Sunderland with ten years at Wolverhampton Wanderers. He was an ever-present in the black country too, winning the Championship title in 2009 and making 33 appearances the following campaign as Mick McCarthy guided Wolves to 15th place in the top flight. 24 goals and nearly 600 career appearances later, Jody hung up his boots and picked up a paint brush, but more of that later.

Jody started his professional career young and wasn't much older when he left for Sunderland. It was a big move for someone of his age.

'I was a young lad at Cambridge, I joined when I was 18 and stayed there until I was 22. I went up to Sunderland for a two-week trial and I was fortunate enough to land a contract. It was a no-brainer really, as a young lad in the game wanting to make an impression.'

Playing a part in a play-off final at Wembley is always a big occasion for any player, but Jody played a part in one of the most infamously cruel play-off defeats in football history. He talked of what the dressing room was like after the penalty shoot-out defeat to Charlton Athletic in 1998.

'It was flat. It's what you would expect after getting beat on penalties at Wembley. You'd worked hard all season to give yourself an opportunity. For myself, it was a fantastic achievement to get to Wembley from where I had come from. It was a great achievement to get to play at Wembley. You just need to learn and build on an experience like that.'

It was a long journey back to the North East for the Sunderland squad after this match, but Jody said the manager and one of his fellow defenders did their best to make sure the heads of all the players involved were kept up.

'We were already booked in somewhere to stop at a function room, so we did stop off somewhere. We had a meal there and a few drinks. It's not what Peter Reid did that I remember it's what Richard Ord did. He wasn't playing but he still did his upmost to cheer everyone up and make everyone feel the best about themselves. That's what was needed.'

He added that the time given to step away from football was vital, and to some extent it helped to press the refresh button. Only then could a team switch back on and prepare for the season to come.

'It was a case of going through the motions then getting home and going away for a time. It's important to have down time and switch off before you need to start thinking about football again.'

Peter Reid was in charge of the club for many years, in which he got Sunderland to the top half of the Premier League. Jody said that he knew he had a good relationship with his old boss because of the trust he had in him to go into the starting XI.

'I feel I had a good relationship with Reidy. He brought me to the club, he's the one who gave me my opportunity and he trusted me to play for Sunderland in the Championship. I was only a young lad, but he had the belief in me. I worked my socks off as much as I could, and he had the faith that I could go on the pitch and perform well.'

Jody said that despite already having some experience at Football League level, he still saw it as a compliment that Peter Reid trusted him at this higher level.

'I'd already been at Cambridge, but this was a new level and he trusted me to make the step up. You need your manager to believe in you to go and do a job on the pitch.'

The defensive solidarity of Sunderland helped to make them a team very hard to break down through the late 1990s and early 2000s. Jody said that his defensive partnership with one player helped himself and the team to thrive, making Sunderland a team that few sides wanted to face.

'Darren Williams, Daz, could play anywhere, I was a good mate with him, so we had a good relationship anyway. He's a player who I feel I worked alongside with well. You need to strike partnerships across the pitch. Two centre-midfielders, right-back, right-midfield. You need good partnerships everywhere. When they work it makes things a lot easier for everyone.'

Sunderland haven't reached the heights of the Peter Reid era since Jody's time at the club and, in reality, have never really come close.

However, any speculation that the team overachieved by reaching the top seven of the Premier League in those back-to-back campaigns was swiftly quashed by Jody.

The way in which Reid's Sunderland side set up to play football made them an intensive unit which would get in the face of any side they came up against. They were hard working and didn't give any opposition side, no matter where they were in the table or what predicament they were in, an inch.

Jody said, 'I don't think we overachieved, we worked very hard to achieve what we did in those two seasons. It wasn't a fluke in any sense because of the type of football we played. We achieved exactly what we worked for.'

There was a fearless edge to Sunderland's game over the period in which Jody was at the club. Many of the big sides in the Premier League would come up against Sunderland and be unable to play their natural game. This, according to Jody, made Sunderland into a stand-out team.

'You win a game and it builds confidence. Teams start to look out for how you are playing. We made ourselves difficult to play against. That's how we would play against teams, we would shut them down right from the off.'

The central-midfield positions are sometimes referred to as the 'engine room' of a football team. If the players in these positions work hard and don't let anything past them, it usually leads to success.

With that Sunderland team, the engine room was filled with the ideal kind of players for the team Reid wanted to build. It also made Jody's life, as a defender, much easier.

'I remember standing in defence and thinking this is making my life easy, from the way our midfield players, the likes of Alex Rae, Stefan Schwartz and Bally, would keep the pressure up.

'I'd just put the tackles in and play the ball out. It was a great position to be in.'

The attitude and work ethic instilled into the players by Peter Reid has not been seen in a Sunderland team since. You would be hard pressed to find many top-flight teams in the last 20 years to have the kind of high intensity style of play that this team played with.

Jody said that no teams were feared by the side that was on the cusp of European football two years running.

'We were grounded, we worked hard for every point we earned. Success breeds confidence and confidence breeds success, they go hand in hand. The team was confident. When we beat a big team, we would move on and believe we could beat the next big team.'

He pointed out once again that what that Sunderland team of 1999 to 2001 achieved was not lucky, and that the work behind the scenes helped to make the side into the successful unit fans saw every Saturday afternoon.

'Every team that is successful you can go behind closed doors and see fantastic camaraderie. It's not through luck that you become successful, so much hard work goes into making a team successful.'

Jody thoroughly enjoyed his time on Wearside, if he didn't then he would not have spent six years of his career at the club. He spoke of how relegation to the Championship helped seal his move back down south.

'I loved Sunderland. I would have stayed there for the rest of my career. We'd been relegated and when teams get relegated they need to move players on. It's as simple as that, they moved me on.

As it was, Jody was given the opportunity to remain in the top level of English football. It was also a chance to move back closer to his home town of Redditch.

'A team came in for me from the Premier League, offered some money and Sunderland accepted. It's that simple, I didn't really have a lot of say in it but what I will say is that I love Sunderland and I would have stayed for the rest of my career.'

As much as Jody loved his time at Sunderland, he had an equally happy and successful period at Wolverhampton Wanderers. A decade at Molineux to finish his career went well for Jody, who said that it was a move he couldn't turn down.

'As it was, I went to Wolves, spent ten years there and had a fantastic time there. It's one of those things in football, I'm afraid. To turn down a move to a Premier League team would have been naïve from me considering the age I was.'

The defender's decision is one which very few players in that same position would dare to turn down.

'I wanted to play in the Premier League. As any player does, you want to play at the top level for as long as you can.'

As mentioned earlier, Jody followed a path which not many professional footballers have trodden. It wasn't coaching or punditry he turned his hand to, but painting.

Jody admitted that it began as a hobby and then developed during his playing career, beginning at Sunderland where he sold some work to his team-mates and others in the area.

'The painting overlapped. I started painting properly at Sunderland, I never intended to become an artist when I retired but just the more I did, the better it got and the more I sold. I retired in 2014 and I wanted to carry on something I loved and made me money. I love the art and doing the painting, I always have. It's great to have it as a job now.'

When he hung up his boots, Jody never aspired to go into the coaching side of the game at a higher level. Instead, he has helped with children's teams and moved his focus onto creating art.

'I coach one team and I manage two other teams. I do this with my kids' teams, and I love it but I haven't moved on and done anything at a higher level.'

Jody's time on Wearside was enjoyable and it was the experience of locals around the city that helped him to settle in and feel welcome.

'I loved it at Sunderland, I played the day the stadium opened. I remember thinking how friendly the people were. It knocked me back, I went into a local baker and got talking to people. I remember thinking this is fantastic. They made me welcome and I will never forget that. I went through some tough personal times there. I can't speak highly enough of people in the North East.'

It was a big move for Jody, to move away and play his football in the north east of England after breaking into the game down at Cambridge. He fit in well with Peter Reid's plan for Sunderland, which is why he made almost 150 appearances for the Black Cats.

Jody is not one of the first players who springs to mind when Sunderland fans talk about that excellent chapter in their club's history. However, his work ethic and calmness on the ball made him a vital piece of a puzzle that came together as a tough tackling, fighting unit which went toe to toe with some of the best teams in the Premier League.

As much as he loved the North East, the people and Sunderland fans, there was one drawback during his time at Sunderland:

'My only negative is that the weather was horrible. The rain and the wind were rotten, but other than that, it was fantastic. It's a shame, there are some beautiful beaches up there too, just not the weather. Gale force wind everywhere.'

Although he was unable to get to grips with the weather, Jody had a great spell on Wearside. He was a near ever-present for Sunderland, playing in some of the club's highest highs and lowest lows.

It tests a player's ability to bounce back when faced with relegation or a play-off defeat, and Jody was able to move on from both to become a cult hero both on Wearside and then in the Black Country for Wolverhampton Wanderers.

He featured in many of the matches Sunderland fans have been talking about for 20 years, and probably will continue to do so for years to come. The play-off final defeat to Charlton in 1998 is heartbreaking for Sunderland fans and the players who took to the pitch, but the pulsating nature of the 4-4 draw and then penalties makes it unforgettable.

Whether with a football at his feet or a paintbrush in his hand, Jody takes everything he does in his stride. He has made sure that even after retiring from the game, he has been able to continue making his living doing something he loves.

CHRIS MAKIN

Chris Makin was born in St Helens, Lancashire, in May 1973. His journey as a professional footballer began just 30 miles away on the other side of Manchester at Oldham Athletic in 1991.

He was born and bred in Lancashire and in the early days he plied his trade within his home county, but his stand-out performances in these years, which included his first taste of premiership football, gave him attention from the continent.

Five years at Boundary Park, including a loan period at Wigan in the 1992-93 season, awarded Chris a move into Europe. Marseille was his next destination, where he made 29 appearances before coming back over to England and Sunderland in 1997.

Chris left Sunderland in a strong position, and he too would go on to improve during his time on the pitch. His final appearance in a Sunderland shirt came in March 2001, in a 1-1 draw at home to Aston Villa. Sunderland lay fifth in the Premier League and would go on to finish seventh for the second consecutive season.

He moved to Ipswich Town, playing alongside Marcus Stewart, who would make the same journey but in the opposite direction in 2002. Stewart finished the 2000/01 season with 19 league goals.

Chris made ten appearances at the end of that season, with the Tractor Boys losing just twice on their way to a fifth-place finish in the top flight.

After leaving Portman Road, Chris went to Leicester City and then Derby County on loan, playing over 30 times in the 2004-05 season for the two East Midlands sides.

His career path took him further south with each of his last two professional clubs: firstly Reading and then Southampton. In April 2008, at the age of 34, Chris took advice from his doctor to retire from the game due to a persistent injury. In total, he racked up over 400 appearances in a professional career which lasted 17 years.

In 1997 Sunderland were at the start of a new chapter in their history. The Stadium of Light had become their new home after spending almost a century at Roker Park. Chris was to become a part of the first squad to represent Sunderland in the new stadium, a squad that were starting life in the Second Division.

More importantly, his move to Sunderland brought about one of the best partnerships in the club's recent history. It was as important as the goals scored by Kevin Phillips and Niall Quinn. Down the left-hand side of the team, Chris and Nicky Summerbee forged a relationship which went a long way to contributing to Sunderland's success around the turn of the millennium.

For many Sunderland supporters, the squads of 1997–2002 were perhaps the best in their lifetime and without doubt one of the best sides in the club's recent history.

Chris talked of how the decision to leave the French club was not entirely his, but that he could have ended up at many clubs worse than Sunderland. The size of the fan base at Sunderland was a defining factor in Chris's move.

'I was forced into it really by the president of Marseille. But I was lucky in that even though my time was up at a massive club, I was joining another club with big support which was important to me.'

Peter Reid was the man to bring Chris to Sunderland. It is nothing new that his time at Sunderland came to an end because of a fall out with his manager. In past interviews, Chris has talked of how things went sour with Peter Reid.

He has previously talked of the change of direction which Reid wanted to take at Sunderland and it essentially didn't include Chris. He admitted that he never saw it coming but was able to move on with his career away from Wearside.

'I had a fantastic relationship until the famous fallout at Highbury and my career at Sunderland never really recovered from that. However, I played my best football of my career under him so I will always be grateful to him for that.'

The team spirit which Reid installed into the team during the 1997–2002 period was arguably the best in the club's history. Sunderland had some players with real quality, but the chemistry created made the side tick more than anything. Chris acknowledged this, identifying how the club was successful because of quality players and characters in the dressing room.

He said, 'There were so many, especially in those days. We had a fabulous group and we all got on so well. Stand out, not really, but plenty of characters who mixed well on and off the pitch.'

Day-to-day life at a football club makes up 90 per cent of a player's role. Supporters witness such a small percentage of what the players do whilst representing their club. The training ground is the place where players would have the best chance to bond and grow together as a unit. Chris explained how he cherished his time in training whilst at Sunderland.

'Life was a blast because of all those characters. Training was hard and competitive which is what you need but the dressing room was a mad house sometimes. In a good way, of course.'

On the other side of the spectrum, it is entirely possible for players to fall out whilst playing together at a club. It is rare, or if it does occur it rarely comes into public knowledge, and even if it is put into circulation, it rarely does so when both players are still at the same club.

Chris was fortunate, he can't recall having a problem with any of his Sunderland team-mates. If this opinion was held by other team-mates then it surely goes to show, 'I never had an issue with any other player whilst at Sunderland. Not that I can remember anyway.'

Chris talked of the importance of having a squad that is both talented and deep. Sunderland had been pieced together meticulously by Peter Reid, meaning that when Chris was injured the impact of losing him was lessened.

'Reidy built up a very strong set up at Sunderland so if a player was injured or suspended then we had another very good player coming in as a replacement. When I got injured in my first season then Darren Holloway came in and was outstanding.'

Chris enjoyed his playing career wherever he went. He made more appearances on Wearside than at any of the other clubs he turned out for. Shaking off the disappointment of the penalty shoot-out defeat in the Championship play-off final of 1997-98, Chris stepped up to the mark and helped Sunderland storm to the title in the following campaign.

At the time, the 105 points registered were a record. It would be the first of several great seasons for Sunderland.

'I played my best football at Sunderland. Not to say I didn't have great times at other football clubs like Wigan Athletic, where I made my league debut, and Oldham Athletic, where I made my Premiership bow, and where I was for ten years since I was a kid.'

Chris added that he enjoyed playing football wherever he went, especially his French adventure before moving to Wearside.

'Marseille was incredible because it was a huge club and with that cane pressure, which was my first taste of that aspect of football. I also enjoyed spells at Ipswich, Derby and Reading.

'Reidy developed a squad of characters and fighters with some wonderful technical players. But you must win games in football for all of that to come together and we fortunately did. It wasn't luck though; it was good signings and good management.'

The Sunderland side which Peter Reid put together around the turn of the millennium was one of the best seen by Sunderland fans in recent years. The piecing together of a squad is a time-consuming process, yet Chris believed the hard work put in at Sunderland by the players and backroom staff made it worthwhile. It led to a side which was on the cusp of Europe on more than one occasion.

Few players have signed for Sunderland from top European clubs and made it on Wearside. In more recent years, players have joined from Bayern Munich, Lazio and Fiorentina. Some have made the grade or have gone down well at the club, such as Jan Kirchoffs's memorable yet injury plagued time in 2016. Others have struggled and left the club with a very low popularity rating, many of the players departing after Sunderland's back-to-back relegations in 2017 and then 2018 fit into that category.

Although Chris enjoyed his time at Sunderland, it's been established that he was not completely in control of his move to Wearside. His time in France was also one which he enjoyed both professionally and as a place to live. It was a case of mixed feelings when he came back to England, yet things at Sunderland quickly clicked into place.

'I adored my time at Marseille. It's a giant of a football club but I loved that side of it. It's an incredible city as well and I returned there in the summer to show my family.

I was gutted when I left but then I would never have had the opportunity to play for Sunderland so swings and roundabouts, eh?'

The chance to play in a Sunderland side on the up was the silver lining to Chris's moving-away-from-Marseille cloud.

When it comes to regrets, Chris doesn't have many. Only the circumstances that saw him leave Sunderland were put down in this category.

'I only regret the way it ended but that was out of my hands. I believed if you're not wanted then get out and that's what happened at Sunderland.'

Chris was disappointed, but he knew that he left Sunderland at the right time. As it turned out, he would have plenty of things lined up for the coming years. He was honest about the way he felt but Chris knew his future lay elsewhere.

'Once you fall out of favour with a manager it can be difficult to keep an interest with the club.'

It came to a perhaps unnatural end, but Chris carried on his career in similar positive fashion. Unlike many players, Chris moved away from football, and the continent, once his boots were hung up. In fact, he went further afield with a partnership which was formed on Wearside.

A spell in the property business was followed by a call from his old Sunderland team-mate to join him in a unique opportunity overseas.

'I used my money from football to invest in properties in Manchester and I managed them when I retired until a certain Mr Summerbee encouraged me to come and work with him in Qatar. And here we are entering our eighth season of covering the local league in English. I'm very lucky.'

Chris always gave his all at Sunderland and was a near ever-present during the four years he had in the North East. His career has moved him far away from the UK, but he left a lasting impression on English football. Not only was he a part of some of the most memorable campaigns, but he was also a key player in some huge victories at Sunderland.

These matches included both 2-1 victories at Newcastle in 1999 and 2000 as well as the famous 4-1 demolishing of Chelsea at the Stadium of Light. These are matches which will go down in Sunderland folklore, and will be spoken about for years more to come.

I was unfortunate enough to not be able to watch Chris in person, but the impression given by supporters who did watch him in red and white is that he was reliable defensively and made plenty of things happen going forward.

The football which he is now involved in is a long stretch from the Premier League football he once played, but he is still involved in the sport he loves.

THOMAS BUTLER

Thomas Butler became one of many players from the Republic of Ireland to join Sunderland when he was spotted by scouts shortly before the turn of the millennium. A central-midfielder by trade, he was asked to move position and become accustomed to playing on the wing, which he did with success.

Butler was at Sunderland for six years, being loaned out to Darlington in 2000 for a short period. Injuries prevented him from truly nailing down a place in the first team, but he did contribute in one of the club's more important matches in recent years.

The Irishman's time on Wearside came to an end in 2004 and he moved across the border to Dunfermline after a successful trial. His contract wasn't extended any further, so he moved elsewhere, spending the 2005-06 season back in the North East with Hartlepool United.

Almost 40 appearances and two goals, his first in professional club football, made for an impressive campaign for Thomas, but a disappointing one for his club. Hartlepool were relegated to League Two and Thomas was soon to be on the move again, this time down to South Wales, for the start of the 2006-07 season.

Swansea City had, the previous campaign, lost to Barnsley on penalties in the League One play-off final. Butler signed and in this first campaign he played over 30 matches for the Swans. The following season would see the side storm to the title, with Butler playing in excess of 30 matches once more.

He flourished at Swansea City, but Butler learnt his trade on Wearside. He was young when he was first spotted by Sunderland representatives, one of whom happened to be a cult legend at the club.

'For me as a young player, playing in Ireland especially, you usually go away to England when you're 16. Playing football from 6/7 years old, it's like with any young kid, you want to go and play your football in England.

'I went for trials for my national team, which was Ireland, and got in there so I was in the under-15 team. You get a lot of scouts from teams coming to watch those games, and I think Sunderland were one of the first teams to show interest. Pop Robson oversaw the youth team at that point. He came over to watch me play against Northern Ireland I think it was. I did quite well, and he rang me to ask if I would come over on trial.'

Thomas said that the atmosphere upon arriving at Sunderland for his trial was the most welcoming he's had at a club.

'I went in at Sunderland, you can always tell when you get more of a feeling for a place. I could tell it was a family kind of atmosphere for players. I'd been at one or two other trials before then which I deemed as more robotic and not as warm.

'I came over to Sunderland, I did well on trial and then Pop Robson rang my parents to say the club were impressed with how I did and asked if they would like to take me over and offer him a contract. So obviously as a kid it's the best moment you've had in your life so far.'

Footballers are often asked to play out of position at one time or another during their careers, but with Thomas he was moved into an unfamiliar role from almost the very beginning.

'I preferred playing centre-midfield and that's where I was trained and played. I was quite small at the time, but as I got older and pushed my way through the reserves you found that the physicality was just the nature of football then. Big strong centre-midfielders and I was more of a technical player.'

Thomas added that it was assistant manager Bobby Saxton who first moved him into a wider position.

'Bobby said at the time, I had pace then, believe it or not back then, go on put him out on the wing and see what he can do. I went and played out wide and did some basic stuff, I did quite well in isolated scenarios.

'I did better in one-on-ones rather than in the middle of the park where big players could kick lumps out of me. I transitioned to a winger during my time at the club, but I enjoyed playing in the middle as it was where I had played throughout my early years.'

Bryan 'Pop' Robson is a Sunderland legend. He played 164 matches and scored 67 goals during three separate spells at the club in the 1970s and 80s. When Thomas came to the club, Robson was established as the youth-team manager.

Thomas had a lot to thank Robson for and was complimentary about the man who had helped bring him to Sunderland.

'As a young player you have coaches who shape what kind of footballer you're going to be. For me, Pop helped me. He played the game at a high level and learning from him was great. He never overcomplicated things as a coach and he never took away from your ability. He let you play as much as possible, but as soon as you made one or two mistakes he would just try and tweak it rather than change it completely. It's that natural ability that gets you in the door.

'Pop was probably way ahead of his time, even then, whereas if you look around now you see a lot of robotic kind of coaching with people reading from books and telling players to do this because it looks good in a book rather than letting people play.

'Pop was much freer with his coaching and would let players express themselves, which is much rarer these days. From what I have seen, this expression is beaten out of more technical players. We had that luxury with Pop. He would trust you and let you go and play, once you repaid him that was it, you were in his good books.

'Our youth team at the time was strong. I think in the team we had 11 internationals playing. We would finish high up every year; it was a successful time for the youth side during that period.'

When asked if he was a patient coach, Thomas said, 'Yes he was [patient]. I have seen some coaches who micromanage and try and do every aspect of a match and predict scenarios instead of letting players get on with it. You wouldn't have got there if you weren't good enough.

'Pop didn't try to change too much about you. As a player, you were there for a reason. If you had any bad habits, he would pull you up and change it, but change if for the better.

'He would never change the good things you would do. You see a lot of that now as players will do something special but because it isn't in a book or a manual, the coaches kill the individuality.

'Pop let players have that freedom, it was much appreciated. It's rare you get that kind of manager these days, I think a lot of them are Spanish managers who allow creative players to perform and tend to not interfere too much. With a lot of younger players, it gets beaten out of them now.'

It was Peter Reid who gave Thomas his first-team debut, and the Irishman spoke highly of this relationship with his first manager at the club.

'Peter was obviously different to Pop in many ways. Peter had all the pressure of winning games as he was the first-team manager, I think with him everything was simple as well. With Reidy, if you worked hard, and as he wanted you to, he was alright with you.

'He had good structure in the team, and I think the main thing with Reidy was he always made sure there was a team of characters and that nobody would shirk responsibility. Every time you had 11 on the pitch, there were at least seven, eight, nine strong characters. He always made sure his teams had that.

'He was also pretty funny at times, but if you ever got on the wrong side of him or let him down, he would let you know about it. There was never any grey area, he was always very straight. He would let you know his feelings, whether positive or negative. If you weren't doing well, you were out.

'I appreciate that kind of manager. Those in the middle where you aren't too sure where you stand with them are the ones who most players don't really like. Reidy was the opposite; he was good.'

Thomas considered the period under Reid at Sunderland to be one of the best of his career due to who he shared a dressing room with.

'I think that was the best period of banter and togetherness in a group. Like I said, I just think all the characters like Chris Makin, Micky Gray, Bally [Kevin Ball] Nicky Summerbee, Kevin Phillips, Niall Quinn, Alex Rae, Jody Craddock were all good, top players too.

'Having a dressing room like this, before football we would have a bit of a laugh, but then when it came to it the intensity was unbelievable. We would often have players squaring up to each other. That's how intensive even training was, everyone wanted to win. even in a small-sided, training match they would be p****d off if they lost. Those kinds of attitudes to even losing in training and a desire to win translated onto the pitch.'

The loss of the characters in the dressing room without replacing them is what caused the team to faulter, according to Thomas. He was at the club during a period of decline which saw Sunderland finish seventh one season and 17th the next, narrowly avoiding relegation.

'When you lose all these characters from the dressing room and don't replace them, you are always going to struggle. We finished seventh twice and it was maybe one bad recruitment window just after the second of these seasons. That was it, it spiralled and continued after that.

'It massively changed the dynamic in the dressing room. I've seen it before where you can smell fear in a dressing room. We never had that in those seasons.

'We went out and played against the big teams and always felt like we could score past and beat anybody. Don Hutchinson might get one, or Nicky Summerbee, then up top you had Phillips and Quinny. There were goals everywhere.

'Defensively we were solid and then you had Bally. If you weren't up to it or if you were lacking in any other way, Reidy wouldn't need to do anything. Bally was there to have a go at you and get everybody going.

'Unfortunately, recruitment people just miss out on signings. They might look at a player and see he has great statistics on paper but sometimes they don't consider personality, which is massive in football and especially huge in the dressing room.'

Thomas was critical of teams who don't keep a certain type of player within their dressing room. After pointing out this was an issue at Sunderland, he drew upon a more recent example:

'If you look at any teams that are successful, you can guarantee they have good characters. A lot of people talk about Manchester United and why they are struggling now. Well, look at their starting XI. There is probably one player in the side who will open their mouth at half-time and even have a bit of banter.

'They just look like they don't care, you can just see it. It's so obvious and it happened at Sunderland for probably too long without someone sitting down and saying "look why are we struggling? There needs to be a reason," and there are more intelligent people than me out there to sit down and say the next recruitment window we have we need to sign characters otherwise what's the point? That's probably the hardest part of recruitment, signing the right people.

'It's not even replacing them. They probably spent more money and thought "we'll just spend more money", but it doesn't work that way. There are lots of players in League One and Two who are real characters and would probably die to play up at Sunderland.'

Thomas added that another current Premier League club are a fine example of how Sunderland should operate their recruitment strategy:

'Your recruitment needs to be spot on to try and assess a player. That's what makes some teams standout over others. If you look at Burnley, even now, they don't have superstars, but they have an old-fashioned group mentality of all sticking together, eating together and going out together. That's why they are probably overachieving every year. When it comes to the crunch, they dig in.

'Many clubs overlook this when it comes to recruitment, I think it's something that Sunderland need to try and get back to. You can't judge personalities from statistics on a page or a video of the player.'

He noted that he had seen another example of a strong dressing room generating success during his career:

'I had it again at Swansea, we won the League One title by a record number of points, but we only did that because of the good characters and experienced players we had. It's a no-brainer, but so many teams keep on missing it.'

The last manager Thomas played under at Sunderland was somewhat of a favourite on Wearside. Mick McCarthy came in to try and prevent the impossible. Howard Wilkinson had left the club in an horrendous position. McCarthy was in charge for the final eight league matches, all eight ending in defeat; however, relegation to the Championship was nailed on well before he took charge.

Thomas enjoyed his time at the club under Mick. It was unfortunate that it came during one of the darkest periods of the club's recent history on the pitch.

'I really liked Mick. For me it came too late, I felt like my career at Sunderland was finished even then, under the last manager before him who was Howard Wilkinson. If the roles were reversed and I had Mick instead of him, I think I would have enjoyed this period a lot more. I think Mick came in and tried to go back to basics. He tried to get the atmosphere up and the team spirit back and to get the players enjoying football again.

'When he came in, he had a bit of a bump. The team he took over had absolutely no confidence and were down in the dumps.

'It's hard sometimes for fans to hear that because you get p****d off and think you're winding them up. They work 40 and 50 hours a week and you're saying your morale is low and you're playing in an unbelievable stadium. That's the hard part for fans to understand, which is fair enough, but footballers are human beings. Money doesn't come into it if they aren't happy.'

The 2002-03 campaign was record-breaking in the wrong way for Sunderland. The Black Cats chalked up just 19 points and four wins, with their last win being picked up in December. One point from their final 17 matches meant that by the time McCarthy came in, the season was all but over.

On McCarthy, Thomas added, 'I think Mick had a massive job on his hands, but, from my perspective, he was honest. Some weeks I'd come in and be alright and other weeks I'd come in and have a stinker. He'd ring you to ask, "what was wrong? You were s**t today." There was no sugar coating anything, which was brilliant.

'Even now I speak to Mick because obviously he's back with the Ireland job and we've no problems we get on quite well. He was good for Sunderland, like any manager you're going to get stick when you lose games, but overall if you ask players what they think of Mick McCarthy the vast majority would be very positive.'

Thomas feels that McCarthy was given harsh treatment at his last league management job, Ipswich Town.

He said, 'Even down at Ipswich, they were booing Mick saying he was a bad manager after they got a couple of top-half finishes, and they hated his style of football. They sacked him and then got relegated whilst being shocking.

'I watched Ipswich, and the players were clapping the fans and vice versa, you would never have had that at Sunderland after playing so badly. You would want to get down the tunnel and out of the ground as quick as possible, but down at Ipswich is was all smiles and saying, "Well we still wouldn't have wanted Mick."

'He must have been laughing his head off afterwards, saying what a bunch of idiots. I think it's the pride down there, they would surely have still wanted to have Mick there during that season. Tell you what, if Mick was still there, they wouldn't have been relegated. No way.'

Looking back, Thomas wished he had left Sunderland when Mick McCarthy's predecessor, Howard Wilkinson, was appointed.

'He was good at Sunderland, but I shouldn't have waited to leave when Mick was there. I should have gone as soon as Wilkinson came in. I think that was enough for me, I should have sorted out my injuries and then gone in and said, "Get me on the transfer list and get me out of here."'

Thomas also gave more insight into this mindset towards the end of his time at Sunderland.

'I was a young lad and football can be a lonely game. It has that kind of macho element, especially back then, where if you ask anyone for a bit of advice or help you're perceived as weak. As a young lad you end up bottling up stuff, when it came down to that.

'Most players who leave a club do so on bad terms, but it's usually a player doesn't sign a new contract, or the fans hate him, and he goes somewhere else for money, or they aren't good enough from the word go and they leave. Then there are a small percentage which turn into legends like Kevin Phillips, they are in the minority though.'

Thomas explained what he has done since hanging up his boots, and how he ended up managing a team in black and white.

'I managed Newcastle United ladies' team; I'd have gotten some stick for that. I was doing my coaching at the time to see if I liked it and the opportunity to manage them came up. I did that for about a year, they were struggling for years finishing bottom of the league.

'We tried our best to be honest with them, our job was to make sure we didn't get relegated. I think we finished fourth or fifth from bottom, we did really well considering most weeks there wasn't a full squad.'

He is, however, critical of the attention Newcastle United gave to their ladies' team.

He said, 'I feel sorry for the women's team, they don't get much funding from the clubs. Sunderland do, but Newcastle didn't. All the funding and money came from the players getting it themselves. That was an eye opener to see how much women's football is underfunded and how little interest is shown from the men's professional clubs. It's shocking really.

'It wouldn't take Newcastle much to throw them £100,000 to buy some new kit and bits and bobs, but they don't. It was an eye opener being there, but it was a great experience.'

Thomas, who lives in Sunderland, is now helping players to make the difficult decisions that he himself made during his career.

'I moved on from there and I just started working in sports management. It's agency work but good for me to try and help young players coming in. They are around 16 to 17 years old, who are in a privileged position, but there are lots of obstacles on the way for them. If I got the right help at a certain age, I probably would have had a different career.

'For me, getting into sport management it's to try and stop those lads making similar mistakes which I made as a young player. If you can help clubs and get god players into the team then everything is good really.

'There is no situation that a young player is going to go through which I haven't been through, so from that point of view it's valuable information you give to them. Whether they take it in – some of them don't – I'm sure I probably had the right advice from people but ignored them, thinking I knew better. At least you can be there to give advice to them.

'It was disappointing the way things ended, but it was that type of era. From a young lad who started playing football, if someone told me when I was 12/13 that in a few years' time I'd be playing in the Premier League and playing for my country and in front of 46,000 people, I would never have believed it.

'I probably played one or two bad games and got stick for it, but I also got man of the match a few times. Players are usually harsh on ourselves; we only remember the bad performances.

'I did pick up man of the match in a match against Derby where we needed a draw to secure safety. I set up Kevin Philips for our goal and it finished 1-1. For playing 15/20 games for the club, I probably had one bad in maybe three or four, which still isn't great, but I have seen many players play plenty more bad games in a row.'

On his career at Sunderland as a whole, Thomas viewed it as an important experience, which helped him later in his career.

'The experience there was important. As soon as I went to Swansea, I was settled mentally. I was grateful for Sunderland, if it wasn't for them I wouldn't have been able to play in the Premier League. I never would have met all these nice people or be coached by Pop Robson. My girlfriend is also from Sunderland and I live here now. I have my roots here, it's all good really.

'You always have regrets, everyone does. No one would say no to changing anything in their past if they had the chance. You would change lots of things. When I hear people say they wouldn't I just laugh and say that's a lie, of course you would.

'It was a brilliant experience and a privilege to look back on. To be able to go back on the pitch there. When you retire you can look back at how it was and how passionate the fans were. You don't as a player, you're in a bubble and stick to a routine.'

Thomas added that he was pleased to not have the social media influence when he started off as a professional:

'Players now can't really avoid that because of social media. That was only really getting started back then, we missed out on that … Thank God!

'To have a career past the age of 30, given all the injuries and operations I've had, is up there with miracle stuff really. Football takes its toll on the body. No one cares about this; people don't see it.'

Thomas Butler was a player who experienced the highs and lows of a turbulent period at Sunderland. He saw the heights of finishing seventh in the Premier League, and just two years later the rock bottom lows of a side that registered just 19 points.

His determination to stop players from making the mistakes he feels he made during his career is what has inspired him into his current job role.

PART 3

2000-2005 INTO THE RECORD BOOKS, TWICE, FOR THE WRONG REASON

Sunderland entered the new millennium sitting pretty in the top four of the Premier League, and despite a poor run between January and March they finished seventh. Stand out matches included a 4-1 win over Chelsea at the Stadium of Light as well as a 2-1 win at St James' Park over Newcastle United.

The following campaign Sunderland made a slower start, winning three of their first ten matches. A strong middle third of the season saw the club sit second in January and an improvement on the seventh-placed finish the previous year looked very likely; however, the form dipped slightly again and once more seventh place was achieved. The cup form was also improved, with Sunderland reaching the quarter-finals of the League Cup where they lost out to Crystal Palace at Selhurst Park.

In 2001-02 both the points and the goals dried up for Sunderland. Just 29 goals were scored, which helped push the club to the brink of relegation. The first half of the campaign could have been worse, with Sunderland sitting ninth at the half-way point. However, a run of three wins in the last 18 matches plunged Peter Reid's side to 17th, with a draw on the last day of the season against Derby County needed to secure safety.

Had Sunderland peaked after four years of flying high? The following season would answer that question. The 2002-03 season would see three different managers sit in the home dugout at the Stadium of Light, the club end the season on a 20-game winless run and finish rock bottom of the table. Peter Reid lost his job in November, Howard Wilkinson took over but was sacked in March, and Mick McCarthy was given the unenviable task of restoring pride to a team that had become accustomed to losing.

McCarthy was able to shake off the dismal season in which he had inherited the Sunderland side. The summer of 2003 saw many cult heroes leave the Stadium of Light, including Kevin Phillips, Kevin Kilbane and Michael Gray. Sunderland, back in the Championship for the first time in four years, enjoyed a fruitful campaign. The Black Cats reached the semi-finals of the FA Cup, falling short against Millwall at Old Trafford. They also came close to an immediate return to the Premiership but suffered more play-off penalty shoot-out heart ache.

After losing the first leg to Crystal Palace at Selhurst Park 3-2, Sunderland had it all to do at the Stadium of Light. They won it 2-1 on the night, with goals from Kevin Kyle and Marcus Stewart taking the tie to penalties. It was a shoot-out that the visitors would win 5-4.

However, like with the shoot-out defeat against Charlton in 1998, Sunderland picked themselves up and made sure they wouldn't need to use the play-offs to get out of the Championship by winning the league.

It was a shaky start to the 2004-05 campaign, with just one win in the first six. However, pieces soon clicked into place in Mick McCarthy's side. After mid-October, Sunderland dropped no lower than sixth place and couldn't be removed from the top of the league for the last eight rounds of matches. Marcus Stewart top scored with 17 goals in all competitions, and Sunderland were back in the big time.

For the second time in three years, Sunderland broke the record for the lowest number of points registered in a Premier League season. Things started badly and got worse for Mick McCarthy and his players, losing the first five, then winning just one of their first 21 matches. It was a bleak time to visit the Stadium of Light as a home supporter, but away fans from 14 of the 19 visiting teams that season would leave Wearside happy and with all three points.

In fact, it would be the final home game of the season where Sunderland would finally pick up all three points, with Antony Le Tallec and Chris Brown scoring in a 2-1 win over Fulham. By this time, Mick McCarthy had been sacked as manager; much more change was to come in the summer of 2006.

MATT PIPER

Born in Leicester in 1981, Matt Piper grew up playing football at a youth level for his home-town club. He made his competitive debut for the first team in the 2001-02 campaign, appearing in a 6-0 home defeat at Leeds United in the League Cup.

After playing in a 4-1 defeat to Liverpool, Piper went on loan to Mansfield Town, where he scored his first senior goal against Swansea City. In January 2002 Piper returned to Filbert Street and played 27 times. He sealed his name in Foxes folklore by scoring the final league goal at Leicester's old ground.

Following Leicester's relegation to the Championship, Piper joined Sunderland for £3.5 million. He had a bright start to his career on Wearside, but unfortunately it would be an injury-plagued stay at the club.

In the 2002-03 season, one which was record breaking in all the wrong ways, Piper made 14 appearances. He featured in derby defeats at Newcastle and Middlesbrough as well as a 3-2 victory at Arsenal in the League Cup. Numerous operations resulted in Piper missing much of the 2003-04 and 2004-05 campaigns through injury. Following on from Sunderland's promotion back to the Premier League, Piper found his opportunities limited.

His final appearance for the Black Cats came in a 1-0 victory over Cheltenham Town at the Stadium of Light, at the beginning of what was to be another season to forget for SAFC.

For Matt, the decision to join Sunderland was made easier by a visit to the area. Taking in the surroundings of two clubs who were after his signature allowed Piper to decide where he wanted to make his next step, although it was hard to leave his home-town club.

'In truth, I didn't want to leave Leicester City, I had only just got into the first team. Having said that, SAFC came in for me along with Southampton FC and the reason I chose SAFC is because I visited both clubs, I had a much better feeling about the area and the people I met when visiting SAFC.'

'The contract offered was longer and a better weekly wage, but my overriding decision was based on the positive warm welcome I received from the club when I first visited.' Money and the faith the club had in him were both key factors for Piper, but the initial positivity shown by those at the club helped the midfielder to make his decision.

Matt was signed by Peter Reid in what would ultimately be the manager's last season in charge of Sunderland after a successful period. It was Reid who was the

most influential factor in Matt joining the club. He wanted to carry on the solid start he had made in the top division with a move from the East Midlands to the North East. The manager at the time, who was Peter Reid, was the main influence in me joining the club.

Piper was troubled with injury through much of his career in Wearside, and it was the repeated problems that would affect him later in life. He admitted that the time on the treatment table was harder than any on-field issues during his career.

He said, 'Probably the most difficult thing I've ever had to do in my football career. When you are nearing fitness again, you start to have very positive thoughts and thoughts of belonging again and as soon as you get injured again you must restart the whole process. The toughest thing is the mental side of trying to remain positive in the face of adversity.'

Matt has often spoken about his struggles with the psychological impact of being able to do your job because of injury. His words have helped others and he has come out of the other side a stronger person.

Matt feels lucky that he was able to represent two sets of passionate supporters. He had an expected, ingrained love of his home-town club of Leicester City, but he was just as positive when talking about supporters at the Stadium of Light.

'I was blessed to have two wonderful football clubs in my career. Both Leicester City and SAFC are wonderful clubs with such passionate fans. For me, the passion and dedication from the fans is what stands SAFC out as a club that is different from most.'

Matt spoke of the hopes and expectations he had when signing for Sunderland. Despite these changing over the course of his career, he didn't regret anything that happened in his time at the club.

'When I first signed, I wanted to achieve a regular starting place and help the team to achieve a mid-table finish. As time went on, I really wanted to win the FA Cup with the club. I thought that dream might be a reality, but we were beaten by Millwall in the FA Cup semi-final at Old Trafford.'

The playoff semi-final defeat to Millwall is a fixture that was hard to swallow for most Sunderland fans, it also saw Tim Cahill score the first of several important goals against Sunderland as he started his career-long purple patch against the Black Cats. This semi-final was hard to move on from as a supporter; as a player it would have been equally as hard.

Footballers are often queried about their frame of mind during big matches in their career, but they spend a lot more time on the training pitch in this more closed-in environment of the club.

At Sunderland, Matt felt that he benefitted from the different characters he came across whilst being on the books at Sunderland.

'The training ground was a brilliant place to be. There were lots of different personalities that on the whole pretty much all got on with each other. The banter between players and staff was excellent and it was a place I loved being in and around, even when results on the pitch were not great.'

This last point here is important. It was interesting to see that the morale of a side, which was relegated with 19 points in one campaign during Matt's time at Sunderland, was not affected by the constant poor performances on the pitch. Some would argue that maybe the players didn't take their situation seriously enough; however, this was not the case according to Matt.

At this time in their history, Sunderland didn't have the strongest of squads, yet Matt confirmed that there were powerful characters in the dressing room.

Some of these characters left a lasting impression on Matt, even when compared with his wider career at other clubs.

When asked about picking out any individuals, Matt said, 'Sean Thornton was the standout figure in the dressing room. He was loud, funny, unpredictable, a constant joker, which can get annoying at times but a very likeable character. He was also a very talented footballer.'

Matt was very unfortunate throughout his career with injuries. The problems began at Sunderland during one of the worst campaigns in the club's history. He, perhaps understandably, doesn't have fond memories of the 2002-03 season. It was perhaps unsurprising that Matt outlined this as the worst campaign of his playing career.

'Personally, it was awful because it's when my knee injuries first started and as a team we were relegated, so bad-all-round season that was definitely the worst of my career.'

Matt was at Sunderland during the last days of Peter Reid's tenure at the club. Reid oversaw some of the best seasons Sunderland had in their modern history, yet towards the end relegation to the Championship looked inevitable.

The capitulation from two seventh-place finishes to then scraping up on the last day of the season in the 2001-02 campaign, to finishing rock bottom of the league 12 months later ranks highly amongst some of the most spectacular in Premier League history.

The man who replaced Peter Reid, Howard Wilkinson, is a man whose appointment divided opinion. Truthfully, amongst Sunderland fans, and with the benefit of hindsight, most feel it was the wrong appointment at the wrong time in the club's history.

Matt fell into this category, feeling that the timing or Reid's departure was far from ideal and that his successor was not the right man to come in and steer a squad low on confidence away from the relegation zone.

'In my opinion, Peter Reid was sacked too soon and the recruitment of Howard Wilkinson was the wrong appointment. He wasn't the type of character to motivate the players and give them confidence to successfully navigate a relegation battle.'

His opinion has support when statistics are brought into the equation. Under Howard Wilkinson, Sunderland picked up just four wins in 27 matches, and only two of these came in the league. It was form that would condemn any team to relegation and, even worse, the record books.

The poor run under Wilkinson cost him his job with almost two months of the campaign still to play, leaving his successor with a team that had no confidence and no form to speak of.

That man was Mick McCarthy, who would take Sunderland straight back to the top flight just two years later. In March 2002, however, he was given the almost impossible task of keeping a struggling side up. It would have been the greatest of miracles and ultimately Sunderland would lose all nine of their remaining league matches, scoring just two goals in the process.

Despite this, his later success at Sunderland will be remembered fondly, as well as his attitude to managing and the ability to do so on a tight budget.

Mick McCarthy is always looked upon as a manager who speaks the truth, to the extent that he wouldn't call a spade a spade but rather an implement to dig a hole with. Despite the disappointing displays on the pitch, McCarthy is remembered with fondness by a lot of Sunderland fans. Matt seemed to share this opinion, respecting McCarthy's approach to management and how he made himself available and approachable for the players in his squad.

'Mick McCarthy was a brilliant manager. He was very tough, blunt and honest, but that's the kind of manager a lot of players respect. He always had time for a chat as well and I really respected that.'

Despite the injury-hit career on the pitch, Matt has since moved on to teach others of his experiences. Dabbling in both coaching and media, he is enjoying how his retirement is going, putting a considerable amount back into the game from the training pitch and from within the press box.

'I'm now a football coach and have started my own Football BTEC academy (The Football & Sports Diploma Academy) in Leicester. I also co-commentate for the BBC on LCFC games home and away.'

Despite being injured throughout most of his Sunderland career, Matt enjoyed his time on Wearside. He was grateful for his time at the club and he was humble about how his career played out. Many players would not have been so positive if their careers at the club had followed a similar path.

Matt said, 'I wouldn't change a thing in my time at SAFC. I absolutely loved my time there, albeit I was injured a lot, but that was something that couldn't be helped.'

Other players who suffered as many injuries as Matt may not have been so positive. He has had his issues with mental health, but Matt has come out a very strong and positive individual.

Matt Piper is perhaps one of the more unfortunate players to play for Sunderland. His injury-hit time was interspersed with just 26 appearances across a four-year period.

His career never really got going due to the injuries that plagued him throughout, but his attitude towards how he played and what he has done since retiring is remarkable. He is enjoying both the coaching and media side of the game, and no doubt he will continue to do so for years to come. He is a prime example of how looking for the positives in any situation is often the best route to take.

Regardless of how his career went, he can look back on it with pride. He played for his home-town club and scored in Leicester's last-ever match at their old home, Filbert Street. He came to Sunderland and gave his all whenever he could. No doubt the lessons he teaches the next generation of players will be of great importance.

CHRIS BROWN

Chris Brown was born in December 1984 and started his youth career with Manchester United. After a move to the Sunderland academy, Chris put the work in and, following a loan spell at Doncaster in 2003-04, made his first-team debut; scoring twice in a penalty shoot-out cup defeat at Crewe Alexandra in September 2005.

Four years, 66 appearances and nine goals later, as well as a loan spell at Hull City during the 2005-06 campaign, Chris made his first permanent move since turning professional. He joined Norwich City, scoring once in 18 appearances for the Canaries. Chris really found his feet when he moved to Preston North End in 2008, playing over 100 times at Deepdale during a three-year period.

In 2011 Chris made a permanent move to Doncaster, the club for whom he had made his league debut and scored his first league goals for. He scored 19 times in over 80 appearances, helping the team to the League One title in the 2012-13 campaign. Chris also scored nine times in the following season in the Championship. From 2014 to 2016, Chris moved to Blackburn Rovers, where he played over 40 times. He signed for Bury for the start of the 2016-17 campaign, but injury prevented him from making any appearances.

Like with many footballers, it all began at Manchester United for Chris. He talked of how he played and trained in Manchester whilst living and going to school in the North East.

'It was a strange one, I was at Manchester United in the school of excellence from the age of eight. My coach up there, obviously we had a training base in the North East, he was Ged McNamee who used to do the north of England for Manchester United.

'I stayed there probably five or six years, to the point where I was travelling down on a Friday afterschool, staying in digs and training and playing games, then travelling back up on a Sunday night for school on a Monday.'

Despite potentially living the fantasy of many people his age, Chris admitted that it was more of a nightmare whilst on the books of the Red Devil's.

'You would think that would be every kid's dream, to do that every weekend playing matches in Manchester United, but I hated every single second of it. I just didn't feel part of it, my confidence hit rock bottom, I just wasn't the same player I knew I could be.'

Chris's father, Alan Brown, was also once an established footballer who also played for Sunderland. Chris said that it was intervention from Alan that began the sequence of events that saw him move away from the North West and back closer to home.

'It was actually my Dad; he came down one weekend to watch me. He spoke to me after and said "you're going to have to get out of there. You look a completely different lad, you're not yourself here or at home. I've just been to watch you play and you're short on confidence."

'So it was that which made me go for it. I spoke to my coach and said that I wasn't enjoying my football there and I needed to get away. Long story short, Ged McNamee had left Manchester United at this point and had gone to Sunderland at the academy.

'He was straight on the phone and asked me to come in and train, to get my love of the game back. It was honestly my first session, I think I trained with the under-14s or under-15s, and I absolutely loved it. It's where I wanted to play my football, I don't know if it was because I was back at home, with familiar accents and familiar faces, but I know that if I had stayed at Manchester United I would have been released and I don't know what would have happened next.'

Chris was grateful for his father's intervention, saying that he felt under pressure to enjoy the situation he was in because so many children his age would love to be in that position.

'It was a blessing. I wouldn't have said anything. What I said before about it being every young lad's dream, I was thinking about that all the time, thinking that people would give their right arm to do what I'm doing. I knew deep down that it wasn't for me.

'I felt like I would be ridiculed if I said anything, I would have stuck with it and gotten released just to say I had done it.'

Upon moving to Sunderland, Chris noticed that he instantly felt more comfortable with his life and his game.

'It's something which I'll always be thankful to my dad for, he probably knew the situation, knew the position I was in and took it out of my hands a little bit. It was a blessing because I hit the ground running as soon as I went to Sunderland, I always felt I progressed, and I always knew that was the best place for me to be playing.'

Before making his debut for Sunderland, Chris joined Doncaster Rovers on loan, who were in the Third Division of English football at the time. It was a fruitful period, with Chris scoring ten goals in 22 matches, helping Donny to lift the title come the end of the season.

When asked about the loan spell in relation to how much impact it had on him making his Sunderland debut, Chris said, 'It was one of the best things I did. One of the main things was that Mick McCarthy doesn't really play youth players. If you look at his track record, there aren't many instances where he has thrown young players in. You need to earn his trust, once you do this, you're in. There's no coming back.

'I needed that. I was playing in the reserves and doing quite well and I could have been playing in the reserves for three years because I wasn't in the first team and able to give the impression I needed to.

'I went to Doncaster where I was playing in the league at a decent level, playing in games which matter to people and games where fans have paid to come and watch. People's livelihoods were on the line.'

His time at Doncaster was carefully monitored by Mick McCarthy, as was shown in an interview the Sunderland manager gave when Chris was playing in South Yorkshire.

'I knew that if I could do the job there, I would earn the trust of Mick. I remember him doing a newspaper article, and I think one of the first-team players had been called up to play for Ireland. One of the journalists asked are you going to watch – I think it was Gary Breen or whoever, I'm not 100 per cent sure – playing for Ireland? Mick replied, "No I'm going to watch Chris Brown play for Doncaster against Macclesfield."'

No sooner had Chris started firing at Doncaster, he was told by McCarthy that he would be involved at Sunderland in the 2004-05 campaign; a season which would end in more silverware.

'Straight away I got his attention. I did well on my debut and then the next week he came to watch me. I think I had a conversation where it was confirmed I would be there until the end of the season and then I would be involved at Sunderland.

'As far as kick starting not only my Sunderland career but also my career in general, the move to Doncaster was the best thing I did. I would recommend that to anybody coming through, anyone who has kids in the same boat.'

This chance to get his first-team debut for Sunderland came just weeks into the new season. Chris started and scored twice in a league cup match away at Crewe Alexandra. The game finished 3-3 but Sunderland lost on penalties, but it was a positive for Chris on a personal note.

Despite the enjoyable debut, the weeks leading up to the match were some of the most up and down of Chris's career.

'I'd been suspended for a couple of weeks before and I felt a million miles away from the first team. It turned out that there were a few first-team players who were injured and so Mick didn't want to risk them in the cup game at Crewe.

'I got called in by Mick into the training ground and he sat me down. He asked if I had been keeping myself fit. I said, "yes," and he said "Great, you're playing tomorrow night against Crewe at Gresty Road. I couldn't believe it. From then on, I was a nervous wreck.

'One of the main things was that I hadn't trained; personally the game couldn't have gone any better. I think I scored two goals but we ended up losing on penalties. It was great for me to earn the trust of the manager, that was brilliant. He repaid that; I think I played on the Friday against Leeds at Elland Road.'

It was this league trip to Leeds which made Chris realise what playing professional football was all about and how it would feel.

'That's when I thought, this is proper football. Growing up, this is what you want to do. Playing in front of a full house on a Friday night, and we beat them 1-0. That two-and-a-half-week period was one of the most up and down of my career.

'It was probably for the best; I knew that I had a point to prove. If I had a nightmare it would have been held against me. You find inner strength from somewhere to think, "Everyone is expecting me to have a nightmare, everyone knows I haven't trained in two weeks, but I want to make a statement." I like to think I did that.'

Chris had already spoken highly of him, but he spoke in further detail of his relationship with Mick McCarthy, and how he had a tough, practical way of getting Chris to use his natural ability on the football pitch.

'My relationship with Mick was brilliant. At that age, 18/19, bear in mind I'm 6 ft 4in, I never used my height or physical presence. As you know, Mick loves a target man, a big striker. I never classed myself as that. I preferred to get my ball into feet and link up the play, but he used to be on my case every single day.

'At the time I would think he's got the hump with me or he's had a falling out, because it was that bad. It was relentless, to the point where he would join in training as a centre-back and every time the ball got played into my feet he was taking me out from behind with the sole purpose of toughening me up.'

Chris said that it took him some time to appreciate what Mick was doing for him, and he appreciated that his manager never gave up on him.

'If I didn't win a header, he'd be saying afterwards what he wanted me to improve on and what positions I should take. He took a real interest in my development and at the time I didn't appreciate it. It's only years later, when I look back, I realised that if he never said anything to me it meant that he'd given up on me. He wouldn't have progressed me to that level.

'The fact he was on my case, kicking me up a height, giving me a bollocking every day in training, meant that he cared, and he felt that I could do a job for his team.'

The 2004-05 season was a positive one for Sunderland and Chris. The club won the Championship title, and Chris was given his chance to further show Mick McCarthy what he was capable of. Although he didn't play week in, week out,

Chris became a prominent feature of the Sunderland squad in the final matches of the season.

'That relationship went on right the way through. He didn't always play me every week, and what stands out for me is the last few games of the promotion season. I was a bit-part player for the majority, and there were two games in a row where I came off the bench and scored, that was Coventry and QPR. I came on against QPR in the first half, I remember coming on for Jeff Whitley. After that, I remember I didn't play that well.

'We went to Wigan, I played OK and we beat them. The next couple of games I wasn't great and pair this with Stephen Elliott coming on and scoring, I'm thinking I'm going to get pulled out of the team.'

Despite thinking that he may not get much more game time in the remainder of the season, Chris's mind was put at ease at the training ground by his manager.

'I always remember one morning walking down the corridor and Mick pulled me over to one side and said, "Browny, you've been absolutely outstanding. Don't worry if you have bad games, you're at that age where you're still learning. You're going to be in my team for the rest of the season."

'Bearing in mind this is a team that is trying to get into the Premier League, playing matches which couldn't matter anymore, and he's taken the time to give me that faith where he probably saw my head was dropping a bit. To hear that was incredible man-management.

'He was true to his word. I think I played every single game after QPR right the way through. We had West Ham, Stoke, Leicester. I think it might have been six or seven games. To hear that during a promotion push to the Premier League it was just unbelievable. That's why everyone says he's the best they have played under.'

The success of that season would have felt a million miles away for Sunderland fans once the 2005-06 season got under way. It was a tough campaign, and one which Chris began on loan at Championship side Hull City when he saw that he would be pushed down the pecking order at the Stadium of Light.

'I went on loan at the start of the season. Mick signed Jon Stead, Andy Gray and maybe somebody else. He also had Steven Elliott still there as well. I wasn't going to feature; I was still young. He felt that my development would happen elsewhere, playing for a team at a good level. So, I went to Hull City for that time.'

However, not for the first time in his Sunderland career, Mick McCarthy stepped in to put an end to a disappointing spell on Humberside for Chris.

'Things at Hull didn't go to plan, and this sums Mick up. There was one particular game where I wasn't involved at all. I travelled down to Reading and I wasn't even on the bench. It was at about ten past two on the day of the match, sat on the bus.

'My phone rang, and it was Mick. He asked, "Are you not involved at all today"' and I just said, "No he's left me out altogether". He then said that he was going to call me back, saying that he wanted me back in on the Monday.'

Two days later, Chris was back at Sunderland and starting against the reigning European Champions at the time. It was stark contrast to sitting in the stands at Reading just five days earlier.

'I went back, and we had Liverpool on the Wednesday night at the Stadium of Light and I started. It's one of the things I think about now. He went out of the way to try and help me, even if it was just to get my confidence up.

'He didn't need to bring me back from Hull and, to be honest, I probably wasn't good enough to play at that level. But it wasn't for the sake of trying, and it wasn't for the sake of my manager not doing the best for me.'

As Chris was out on loan, his first taste of the 2005-06 campaign at Sunderland was this Liverpool match at the end of November. At this point in the season, Sunderland sat bottom of the table with just five points and only one win to their name.

He admitted that the team were aware they weren't good enough for the top flight, but that they always put in as much as they could to every match.

When asked what it was like to re-join Sunderland mid-way through such a tough season, Chris said, 'It was hard to come into. We kind of knew we weren't good enough; I don't think the players who were brought in were as strong as we already had. There might have been pressure to play them.

'In terms of characters in that dressing room, I wouldn't have swapped them for anyone. They were honest and they gave their all for their teammates and the manager. It came down to the simple fact that they weren't good enough. There was no criticism of the manager, no bickering in training, everyone wanted the same thing we just weren't good enough to achieve it.'

Chris scored one goal in the Premier League, and this came in the club's final home game of a turgid season. A 2-1 win over Fulham prevented a full season without a victory at the Stadium of Light, whilst at the same time condemning the West Londoners to a campaign without a win on the road.

Chris talked of the relief for the caretaker-manager in charge of Sunderland at the time, but also the embarrassment that came with such a lowly home tally of wins.

'I think a lot of us were really pleased for Bally [Kevin Ball]. He was caretaker-boss at that time, for me personally he was unbelievable. I think I played in every game which he was in charge of.

'There was some relief, but it was embarrassing. Even getting only one home win was embarrassing, it's just not as bad as getting none, obviously. It was nice to get that monkey off our backs and to give the fans something to cheer about.'

Despite the poor season, Chris pointed out that there were some enjoyable nights that season. In April, Sunderland went to Old Trafford to face Manchester United. The Red Devils needed a win to keep in the title race. Although the 0-0 draw was enough to confirm Sunderland's relegation, Chris viewed the match with pride.

'We had some good nights in the Premier League. I remember Old Trafford where we got a point when they needed to win to stay in the title race. Looking back on games like that is, from a personal point of view, unbelievable.

'I remember sitting in the changing room after the Fulham game and thinking I was never going to be a Premier League player, but that no one can ever take away that one Premier League goal I scored. I still feel that way now, I'm still proud. Even though it was a s**t season, I didn't feature much, I can look back and say I scored a Premier League goal.'

The following summer was one of huge change for Sunderland. A new owner, a new chairman and eventually a new, long-term manager. Chris said that things were all over the place until Roy Keane was appointed in August.

'Pre-season was a shambles. We went to Bath University and the physio took all the sessions because we didn't have a manager at the time. I don't think there were a lot of signings at the start of pre-season, just because the club was up in the air. I know Clive Clarke signed at some point, as well as Robbie Elliott.

'It was only when Roy Keane came in that there was an influx of big-name players. Roy Keane agreed to the job, but he wanted a few weeks to have with his family. That's when Niall appointed himself as manager.

'That was a disaster, we were bottom of the table at this point. I managed to get myself back into the team and into Quinny's reckoning. I played a couple of games and there was talk of a new contract.'

Despite working his way back into the squad, Chris saw the signing of a new contract by one of his fellow strikers and the signing of another forward as decisions that would see his future lie away from Wearside.

'However, the thing that went against me was that Daryl Murphy had just signed a long-term deal a couple of months beforehand, with us being similar players in terms of build and attributes.

'Even though there was talk of me getting a new contract, when Keane came in I just had a feeling that it wasn't going to happen. He was bringing in these other players, like David Connolly and then later, after I left, Stern John, I just had a feeling my days were numbered.

'Even though I started in his first match, I just had a feeling. His record spoke for himself that season though, it was great.'

When Roy Keane was appointed manager, it signalled the beginning of a wave of new signings. When Chris talked about Roy, he did so with admiration, feeling fortunate to have a good relationship with him.

'It was brilliant with Roy. He was on my case about my game, but he always had time for me. He didn't have time for many players at that time, he had a real go at some, but for some reason he always had time for me.

'The day I left, he left me a message wishing me all the best. My relationship with him was fine, it was just a case of me not being good enough for where he wanted the club to go. He was honest and I respected him for that.'

Chris's time at the club came to an end in January 2007, with a move down to Norwich City. He said that his reasons to leave Sunderland were based on the realisation that he wouldn't get the chance to play much football, so he went elsewhere to achieve this.

'I think I realised that the club was on the up and that my time was limited, but I also wanted to play football. I wanted to go to another club and get games, so I moved to Norwich, which was five hours away. It was probably a daft decision in hindsight, but it was a purely football decision.

'As far as my relationship with the club went, it was fine. It was just a purely football-based decision to leave.'

Chris was at Norwich for a relatively short period, before moving across to Lancashire and Preston North End. He said that his success at Deepdale was down to the work of the club's physio at the time.

'I went on to Preston after that and I had my best year over there. I struggled a lot during my career with back and knee issues, but at Preston the physio at the time knew exactly what to do with me. It helped me to have the best six months of my career. I then went back to Doncaster; it was nice to go back there. It was the same chairman as the first time around so that was good.'

It was this second spell at Doncaster that revealed why Chris was signed up by the Yorkshire club on both occasions.

'It's funny, the only reason he signed me on loan originally was because he was a massive Doncaster fan and he loved watching my dad play. I think my dad was his favourite player, when he heard that Alan Brown's son was coming through the ranks, he wanted to sign me.

'I don't think they even saw me play first. I knew that if I was finishing a contract somewhere, Doncaster would always have me back because the chairman loved my dad.'

When asked if there was anything in his career that he regretted or wished he could change, Chris spoke of an injury which very nearly ended his playing days before they'd properly started.

'You know what, there isn't anything really. I did have a serious injury when I was 18 and I did both cruciate ligaments in my knees and my medial. I went to see a surgeon in Bradford and he said my career was over, that I would never play football again. From then on, I just said to myself that whatever I achieve I'll be grateful.'

Chris has a lot to look back on with pride over his time at Sunderland, and he was able to tick off several of his childhood dreams whilst at the Stadium of Light.

'To get back from a career-threatening injury to getting promoted to the Premier League and then to play in the Premier League, I look back fondly on my time at Sunderland.'

'There are a lot of good memories, like the parade around the city after winning the Championship, playing with some unbelievable players and working under some amazing people like Mick and Bally. Playing for Sunderland is something which I'm very proud of.'

Chris's playing career came to an end in 2017, and he talked of what he has done since, which predominantly includes being one of the founders of the 'Under the Cosh' podcast with other ex-footballers.

He spoke of how he struggled during the first months following his retirement, and how the podcast helped him to vent some of the issues which were on his mind.

'It's just over two years since we started the podcast and about three years since I retired. To be honest, I did nothing for 18 months. It was a tough time; I was out of a routine and I had no real focus. I was struggling and I didn't know what to do.

Luckily, it dropped at our feet that we should start a podcast. I got rid of any demons I have by talking about it every week to other guys we've had on, who have been through similar things. It's helped to talk about my problems, the good times and the bad times, and it has given a bit of structure to my life, more importantly.'

The coaching and management role is perhaps the most trodden path by retired footballers, but Chris said he quickly dismissed this as something he had little interest in.

'Coaching has never really been something I have considered. I think I would struggle with it, unless I'm playing, I don't think I would want to be anywhere near that environment. I think it would make me feel worse rather than better, I don't think it would be for me. People say get your badges just so you have them, but I've never really been bothered about it.'

He added that his decision not to go into coaching has been helped by talking to those who have struggled in the industry.

'I've spoken to people about their experience of coaching, especially in the youth set up, and they wouldn't recommend it. They have walked away from it, because it's thankless hours and not great pay. They can do better, more productive things.'

Chris has always loved Sunderland, and he completed the path of supporter, to player, to goalscorer whilst at the club.

He spoke of his pride in achieving so much at the club he watched week in, week out from the stands.

'I lived my dream at Sunderland. I was a season-ticket holder and I always wanted to pull the shirt on, I always wanted to score at the Stadium of Light and I always wanted to play in the Premier League. I managed to do all that with them. I'm very proud to have done this, to follow in my dad's footsteps by playing for Sunderland. There is nothing but good memories.'

Chris Brown didn't enjoy the most consistent time as a Sunderland player. Suffering a serious injury at just 18 and getting told he would never play football again would be enough to shatter the dreams of almost anyone in that position. But Chris stuck with it, worked hard and became a Premier League goalscorer and league winner at two different clubs.

His time at Sunderland coincided with a rollercoaster period for the club, and as a supporter he would have no doubt known the contrasting emotions in the stands as well as in the dressing room. In the club's recent history, not many players will have enjoyed (or endured, depending how you look at it) this period more than Chris Brown.

ANDY WELSH

Andy Welsh began his playing career with Stockport County, playing over 80 times for the club before the age of 21. A near ever-present at a young age and solid performances rewarded Andy with attention from elsewhere in the Football League.

Sunderland signed the winger in November 2004 after a successful trial. Andy made 25 appearances for the Black Cats, featuring in the promotion campaign of 2004-05, and was a standout performer in the disappointing 2005-06 season that ended in relegation from the Premier League.

After Sunderland, Andy swapped the UK for Canada, where he played for Toronto FC during their first-ever campaign as a Major League Soccer side. One goal and 20 appearances during the 2007 campaign was followed up with a return to England and Blackpool.

It was at Yeovil Town in 2008 where Andy made himself a staple of the side, featuring over 100 times in three seasons for the Glovers. He would later go on to play for Carlisle United and then Scunthorpe United in 2013.

Andy talked of how he started his professional career for the club close to his home town of Manchester, and how he almost ended up staying in Lancashire before Sunderland offered him a trial.

'I was only 16 at the time. I went off for some trials at Huddersfield, didn't enjoy it there, and then I went to Stockport. I was there for five or six years and from there I signed for Sunderland.

'I'd already been at Blackburn – I was due to sign for them – who were in the Premier League at the time, and that didn't materialise. So, I went back to Blackburn and the following week Sunderland were in contact.

'That's how it happened; I was excited for the opportunity. When I first joined Stockport, we were a Championship club, but we had since gone down to League One. To get the chance to go to such a big club in the Championship was something which I relished, it was very exciting.'

Mick McCarthy was the man at the helm when Andy joined Sunderland, and he had things running very smoothly on Wearside. Sunderland would go on to finish top of the Championship. Andy spoke of his relationship with his manager with high praise, comparing him to some of the best managers the game has ever seen.

'It was amazing. Without doubt he was the best manager I worked with in my career. Managers nowadays can no longer lead through fear, the best managers over the past ten years are leading through love. You look at Jurgen Klopp now, all his players and fans adore him. Mick McCarthy was similar in that sense.

'I've never worked with Sir Alex Ferguson, but you see his traits and what he used to do was bring in people around him who could do things that he couldn't do. He would find someone to take over his weaknesses. That's what Mick was good at, not just his understanding of the team but also as the individual.'

Andy said that the reputation that McCarthy had of someone who wouldn't fudge his words was true, saying that his methods were effective and got results.

When asked if this viewpoint was true, Andy said, 'I think it is, but there were a couple of times that I might have gone over the top. He would bring out a player in front of the whole squad if they did something wrong. That's a part of life, if you make a mistake you hold your hands up.'

The praise for his former manager continued, with Andy saying what McCarthy did at Sunderland and then Ipswich with little funding was a success.

'I think overall his personality traits were spot on. I still think now, you look at what he has done with Ireland, he's gone on to do well with them from the position they were in. Every club he's been at he's had success. Ipswich – they missed out a couple of times, but again he had no money there.

'People forget, he had zero money at Sunderland, and he got us promoted to the Premier League with players like me, Dean Whitehead, Liam Lawrence, Chris Brown, who was a young lad coming through. These are all players who have gone on to have good careers.'

Andy made a goalscoring start to his career on Wearside, but he pointed out that finding the net on his first outing for a club became something of a trait for him during his playing days.

'Obviously, it was great. I scored on my first start in the football league. Funnily enough, wherever I went I would score on my first game. It was a bit of a weird one really. I remember it was against Crystal Palace in the FA Cup.'

It was a goal that one team-mate tried to claim as his own, but Andy acknowledged this as being the sign of a determined goalscorer.

'It was a free kick which I've swung in and it missed everyone and went in. I remember Marcus Stewart trying to claim it, like all good strikers do, but obviously it showed on the replay that he was nowhere near it. He got his goal in the end, though.'

When asked if any of his team-mates at Sunderland stood out, Andy said he didn't think they did because they all stood out in their own way. They were a hard-working squad, this being visible from the stands as well as within the dressing room.

'It was the kind of squad we had at the time, there were no superstars. Everyone mucked in and worked hard. I saw Steve Caldwell put something up and I think another of the good trait of not just what Mick did but what he instilled in us as a squad was the accountability, so if we didn't do something on the pitch or in training then we dealt with it ourselves.

'I'm a big believer in the idea that the best teams manage themselves. If you have a good group of players, managers shouldn't need to deal with anything in the dressing room. Sometimes even on the pitch they shouldn't need to manage.'

The season would end badly for the club, but Andy said that there was plenty of optimism in the build up to the 2005-06 campaign in the Premier League.

'The build up for that season was amazing. Even up until the first match of the season, we were all excited obviously. Most of us hadn't played in the Premier League before. The competitive nature of the squad was great. I came back absolutely flying because I wanted to be in the team, so did others. We were all excited to fight for our places.'

It's sometimes difficult to assess how a team's season can go so badly wrong, but Andy said that the answer lay in a simple lack of finances. He did say that he had admiration for the way the club didn't panic buy and throw money around that they didn't have, an issue which has plighted Sunderland on some occasions in the campaigns since.

'No money, it was as simple as that. Our biggest signing was Jon Stead for about £1.6 million. I always go back to it, it's not Mick's fault and it's not the club's fault. I admire the situation because money wasn't thrown at it. We would have been in a precarious position if that had happened. It's ambition, in my opinion there could have been a bit more ambition.

'The signings were potentially all we could get at the time. It's not just about the transfer fees it's also about the wage structure. I think that was a big part of it at the time.'

When it came to transfers and who Sunderland could and couldn't afford in the lead up to the start of the season, Andy used an example of a player who alluded the club during the summer and who signed for Sunderland's opening-day opponents, Charlton Athletic.

'I go back to the first game of the season. All summer there was talk of us getting Kenny Miller or Darren Bent. We didn't get either of them. At the time Ipswich were a decent side. They had Tommy Miller, Kelvin Davis and Darren Bent as their main goalscorer. We got Tommy and we got Kelvin; you can say they are experienced players who could make the step up.

'Meanwhile, Charlton signed Darren Bent. In that first game of the season he was the difference, by a country mile. He had two chances and scored both. It was the first game of the season for us and we lost 3-1, but I remember I set the first goal up and we created lots of other chances, we just didn't have anyone to put it in the back of the net.'

The issue of not having a proven goalscorer to lead the line and the unfortunate nature of losing so many matches by a small margin combined to leave Sunderland rooted to the foot of the table for most of the season.

According to Andy, these two issues haunted Sunderland for most of the campaign. This run started with the second game of the season, which was frustrating personally for Andy.

'This was all through the season, we didn't really get battered. The following week we played at Anfield against Liverpool, who had just won the Champions League, and we only lost 1-0. I got sent off in the 75th minute, I really shouldn't have been, we were 1-0 down at the time and we were by far the better team for large parts of that game. Again, no one to put the ball in the net.

'It's a funny one. It got rescinded, which is great, but when I think back at it I didn't know it was going to get rescinded so I was thinking, "what have I done here?"– my second start in the Premier League, I'd been sent off and I couldn't believe it.

'I remember Garcia spun out of the challenge, he was diving quite a lot that day, and he spun into me and the referee had already given the free kick. I think what happened was I had shrugged him off with my leg and it looked like a kick, but it wasn't. Obviously, he's made a meal of it and the ref has sent me off.'

The frustration came from Andy having a good match up until the point of the controversial sending off.

'I was having a very good game, up against Steve Finnan. I was popping up in holes, causing problems, you just don't know what would have happened. It's all ifs and buts now, but it's those kinds of games you look back on, the game-changing moments.

'You go through the season and you get other games, like at Wigan we concede a penalty within ten seconds, that goes in and we lose the game 1-0.'

Andy talked of another match later in the season which exemplified Sunderland's lack of luck and a proven goalscorer.

'West Ham at home, I remember getting man of the match in that game. Tomas Rebka was the full-back, I remember setting the goal up, but I also remember putting one on a plate for Andy Gray. The ball broke from their corner and I remember Rebka came in from the half-way line and tried to smash me, but I let it go through my legs and I had a full half of the pitch to run into.

'I got to the by-line and dinked a ball into the box to Gray, edge of the six-yard box and headed it straight at the keeper. It was a game-changing moment.

'Also in that game, I scored straight from a corner and the ref disallowed it. He said that someone had impeded the keeper, even though none of our players were anywhere near the keeper, but he disallowed the goal.'

The summer of 2006 saw some big changes in the upstairs of the club. Niall Quinn was the new chairman and, for a brief period, the manager at the club. Andy talked of what that summer was like and how he suffered a serious set-back whilst on the club's pre-season tour of Ireland.

'He [Quinn] came in and said that there is going to be a takeover at the club. We didn't have a manager; we did pre-season down in Bath without a manager. I got injured during the pre-season, over in Ireland, I did my ankle ligament in. That ruled me out for the start of the season, which was a nightmare.

'Niall kept in contact with me, it was just a case of getting the season started. It was a difficult start. I had a few dealings with him, I got on well with him. Obviously, when I left, me and Roy Keane had a bit of a fall out but fair play to Niall he helped to settle it because Roy was unwilling to discuss it further.'

Andy was disappointed in the way that his Sunderland career ended, and he was disheartened with the way he was treated at the club when returning from a loan spell. He felt that his next move away from Sunderland was being dictated by new manager Roy Keane.

'I would have stayed longer, but I didn't feel I was going to get opportunities. I had already been out on loan at Leicester, I came back and was getting told I would need to go out on loan again. Basically, Keane was trying to dictate where I was going.

'He didn't want me on loan in the Championship, he was trying to offer me loans which just weren't going to do. In the end I sat down and said, "I've got this opportunity to go to Toronto FC, can I go out and have a look," and he said, "Yeah sure, go out and look." We couldn't reach a deal at first with Toronto straight away, but eventually we did. I spoke to Roy; we had a fall out because he was digging his heels in about money.'

His experiences of Keane at Sunderland forced Andy to see one of his footballing heroes in an altogether different light.

'I'm a big Manchester United fan and obviously he was a big player for Manchester United and for me growing up, but I lost a lot of respect for him the way he handled stuff. It shows in the press, it's cringey at times. He sells himself as this guy who everyone wants to listen to, the only reason they want to listen to him is because he is quite a horrible guy, the way he speaks on the TV.

'Going back to it, he fell out with Alex Ferguson too. He has no respect for people. I'm not saying he needs to have respect for me but he's calling one of the best, if not the best, manager there's ever been, saying that he isn't as good as people say he is.'

As much as Andy wanted to remain at Sunderland, he went on to thoroughly enjoy his next challenge, which took him over to the then newest league team in the North American MLS.

When asked about his experience at Toronto FC, Andy said, 'I really enjoyed it. It was a new challenge; we were the new kids on the block. The reason why I fancied a challenge is because it's a city which is steeped in history from the NBA with the Raptors to the NHL and the Maple Leafs.'

Andy wanted to be a part of a famous sporting city, and he was so much of a new player that the home of his new team was still under construction.

'We went out there to have a look and even at minus 19 degrees, and I'm talking of the city being absolutely covered in snow, me and my Mrs had a good feeling for it. The stadium was still getting built.

'I fancied the challenge; it was something different and it was a gamble because I was going away from English football. I wanted to because of how badly I felt I'd been treated at Sunderland."

Andy spoke further of the way he felt about the end of his Sunderland days. In somewhat of an exclusive, he said that the way he was treated at the club left him feeling embarrassed.

'To be honest this is probably the first time I've really said this in an interview because I have been trying to come to terms with it, but I felt embarrassed with the way I was treated at Sunderland. It's because of what happened in front of my own team-mates.

'I'd gone to Leicester, come back and then there were three or four of us training. Rory Delap, Clive Clarke, Kenny Cunningham and Steven Wright. The five of us trained on our own with Kevin Richardson. The way we got treated was an absolute joke.'

The frustration of his final season at Sunderland seemed to spawn from the fact he was offered and then signed a new three-year deal in the summer of 2006 thanks to Quinn.

'Going back to Niall Quinn. He offered me a three-year deal in the summer, which I signed. That's why I took issue with it.

'When Roy Keane came in, in all fairness I was injured, but they signed a couple of players which is fine, but then when the time came for me to leave Roy is trying to dig his heels in. I just said how you can't have your cake and eat it. That's exactly the way it was, and I think Niall understood that, but there was no talking to Roy.'

It was clear that Andy had every intention of remaining on Wearside during and after the 2006-07 campaign, but he realised that he would need to move on.

'That was the whole point. I wanted to stay at the club longer, I'd been there two years and I was still only 23. I wanted to be a big part of the club going forward.'

Despite the sour ending to his Sunderland career, Andy was upbeat and generally positive about what he had managed to achieve whilst playing at the Stadium of Light. He was grateful that he was able to achieve things which very few others have.

'It was a fantastic time. I'm a positive person, even throughout the darkest times in a relegation from the Premier League there are still moments from even a season like that. I can always say that I have played in the Premier League, 16/17 times in the Premier League, which is almost half a season. I have great memories. As much as there may have been players since who might go down as heroes, I have been there and done it as part of a fantastic set of players and backroom staff.'

Andy added that one of those sought-after footballing memories was one that had its own controversy on the pitch; and it is a match that no Sunderland fan wants to be on the losing side of.

'Even the season in the Premier League, I have done something which many Sunderland players and fans will never do and that's start in a Tyne–Wear derby at St James' Park.

'There we have another big moment, if anyone wants to watch that one back, it was a flipping embarrassment. I remember picking the ball up on the half-way line and Scott Parker came in and smashed me on the half-way line.

'Two minutes later the same thing happens with Parker and the referee, who knew Parker would have been sent off, decides to book Stephen Carr, who was nowhere near me. It was embarrassing and we went on to lose the match 3-2.'

The match included two superb strikes for Sunderland, two goals which Andy noted would be good enough to win any match. Unfortunately, on that day, the efforts counted for little.

'Any other game, you score two wonder goals from Steven Elliott and Liam Lawrence, and you win. To be honest we should have at least got something out of the game.'

Thoughts turned to what Andy has done since hanging up his boots, starting with his managerial career, which has taken him back up to the north east of England on multiple occasions and pitted him against one of his former team-mates from Sunderland.

'I've been managing a team called Ossett United, who have been up in the North East to play against Morpeth and South Shields. Julio Arca played against us for a couple of seasons too.'

As well as management, Andy is well on his way to building up his coaching career. When we spoke, he was putting on online coaching courses from his own footballing academy for children to take part in during the coronavirus pandemic lockdown.

'I've also got my own academy, so I'm currently doing some free online sessions for children on Facebook. That's what I've been up to. I'm due to finish my A licence, I need to be assessed on that when all of this is over. An ambition is to get as high up as possible in the coaching or managing industry.'

Andy Welsh was a winger who stood out during a tough campaign for Sunderland. it remains to be seen what more he could have achieved on Wearside, but when he did play for Sunderland, he always put a shift in. He could easily have been a key member of the 2006-07 promotion-winning campaign and beyond, but nevertheless he enjoyed his career before, during and after his time at the club.

BEN ALNWICK

As an academy product, Ben Alnwick was at Sunderland from a very young age. He rose through the ranks, making his first-team debut at the end of the 2004-05 season. Ben played in the match that saw Sunderland secure promotion back to the Premier League, as Leicester City were beaten 2-1 at the Stadium of Light.

After three appearances during this season, Ben would be up against the experienced stopper Kelvin Davis as Sunderland went to battle in the top flight. Alnwick appeared seven times in the season, which was disastrous for Sunderland, with five of these being in the league.

Following Sunderland's relegation with just 15 points, Ben was first choice in the Championship up until October, making 11 appearances. As he would be playing behind new signing Darren Ward, Ben looked for a move away from the Stadium of Light.

His next venture would be to Tottenham Hotspur, with the late Marton Fulop coming in the opposite direction. He struggled to break into contention at White Hart Lane, and he went on loan seven times during his five years in north London.

After playing a cumulative 22 times for Luton Town, Leicester City, Carlisle United, Leeds United, Doncaster Rovers and Leyton Orient, Ben joined Barnsley on a permanent basis in July 2012. He played on 10 occasions at Oakwell, as Barnsley narrowly avoided relegation from the Championship.

Ben played for Charlton Athletic and Leyton Orient during the 2013-14 campaign, but it was the following season in which he secured the number one spot.

Between 2014 and 2017, Ben played over 80 matches for Peterborough United. In each of these years, the Posh fell short of the League One play-offs, and in August 2017 he joined Bolton Wanderers.

It was a successful first campaign in Lancashire for Ben, as Bolton achieved promotion and he played 21 times in the league.

The following two seasons he played a further 69 matches as Bolton staved off relegation despite being under a transfer embargo before falling to relegation in the 2018-19 season. Ben left the club and has had a break from football since then; but he is far from ready to retire.

Starting at his early days, Ben spoke of what it was like coming through the academy set up in the late 1990s and early 2000s. In 2003 Sunderland moved their academy to a state-of-the-art Academy of Light, giving them the facilities of a top club.

Ben played at both the old academy set up and the new facilities.

He said, 'It was unbelievable to be honest. When I first went there, it was still the old Charlie Hurley centre, which was just a small training ground, but it had immaculate pitches. It was brilliant.

'Once we moved to the new facility, the Academy of Light, it was a different ball game altogether. At the time, it was probably the best academy in the country and, with the staff who were there, it was unbelievable.'

Ben had been on the bench on several occasions during the 2004-05 season, one that would end in promotion for Sunderland. He was given his debut in the match which sealed this promotion. At the age of 17, it was a dream come true for the man from Prudhoe, Northumberland.

He explained how he felt to play, and how his involvement in the match was very much touch and go.

'It was unreal. The time I got in was at the end of the season, when we were going for promotion. It was Leicester City at home. There were a few injuries, I wasn't sure if the gaffer would pick me though.

'I had been on the bench throughout the season, and we had Michael Ingham there at the time. I'm sure it was Ipswich away, we played Ingy but we got beat. The next game the gaffer put me in. It was unbelievable, to get that chance to play in front of that many fans.'

Despite still being unable to legally buy a pint, Ben had made his debut in the second tier of English football. It was something he was very grateful to Mick McCarthy for.

'It was also great to see that Mick had faith in me, to play at such a young age. It was a dream. I had been at Sunderland since I was 11 years old and I had come all the way through. To make my debut at home as well, it's something I'll never forget.'

Few players have made their first-team debut at the same age as Ben, and from those who have even fewer have first appeared at a level as high as the Championship.

When asked what it was like to make his first appearances at this young age, he said it was a significant help to his career.

'It was beneficial. When you're young, you are just fearless. I wanted to play, even though I was always on the bench, I was always pressing and working to be involved. Fortunately, I was able to get in and play a few games towards the back end of the season.

'We got promoted and it was the best experience I probably could have had at that age. It was such high pressure, so it stood me in good stead. To come through the full season and being involved with the first team, getting the hang of how things worked and then coming in to play.

'In terms of memories made, it was probably some of the best times of my life.'

The following season in the Premier League would go on to be a testing one for Sunderland goalkeepers, with the Black Cats picking up just 15 points. Ben played a part in the season, but he knew that McCarthy would be looking to bring in a goalkeeper with more experience.

'To be honest, I'd played the last few games of the previous season, but I knew I was still very young, especially for a goalkeeper. I wasn't stupid, I knew they would bring someone in.

'Having someone like Mick as the manager, he knows the score and he knew we needed the experience. At the time I was probably too young. I was still only 18 at the time and that's especially young for a goalkeeper.'

'I knew another keeper would come in, but obviously I was still going to fight for my place and progress. It was difficult though. At the time, the team wasn't doing too well. We were struggling, it was a hard time. There would have been a lot of pressure surrounding the staff and the management.'

The senior keeper who Ben expected to join that club was Kelvin Davis, who signed from Ipswich Town.

Ben said that he was a great professional to have around, and that he had sympathy with the way Davis was treated by Sunderland fans throughout the season.

When asked about his relationship with Davis, Ben said, 'It was unbelievable. I remember it was difficult for me at the time getting in that season and eventually playing a handful of games. For me it was a dream to play in the Premier League at such a young age.

'It was difficult for me though; Kelvin wasn't having the best of times. It was hard for me to see such a nice guy, who was smashing and was very good with me and the younger goalkeepers, get so much stick from the fans.'

Goalkeepers notoriously get the most criticism in their role as the last line of defence, and fellow keeper Ben said it was tough to listen to the anger thrown at Kelvin.

'To be fair, he wasn't the only one, but I just felt that with Kelvin they made a beeline for him. Listening to some of the chants and boos towards him, it was hard.

'Obviously at the same time it gave me a chance to play in the Premier League, which is ultimately something I wanted to do at that age. It was tough, but like I say with Kelvin, and all the goalkeepers at the club when I was there, my relationship was great.'

Ben added that all throughout his time at the club, as a senior player and way back to his early days in the academy, he always got on well with the other goalkeepers Sunderland had, whoever they were.

'Even going back to when I was very young and the likes of Tommy Sorenson and Jurgen Macho were there, I still remember them. There was Mart Poom and Tommy Myhre, there was always a good relationship amongst the goalkeepers.'

The life of a goalkeeper can be a hard one, and Ben said that his career so far as a shot stopper has had its highs and lows.

'It is [up and down], it's the rough with the smooth. I did it, I went to Bolton after being at Peterborough for a few years. We were sort of in and around the play-offs at Peterborough. I went to Bolton and suddenly I found myself in a team that was winning and ended up getting promoted. It is a totally different ball game depending on what team you play in.'

Going back to his former team-mate, Ben said that Kelvin showed his ability by going on to have a very successful period on the south coast, admitting that there was a lot of pressure on each player during Kelvin's season at Sunderland.

'Kelvin left Sunderland and he went on to Southampton and they went from League One to the Championship, then to the Premier League. He carried on playing in the top division, showing that he wasn't a bad keeper. It's just when he was at Sunderland, there was a lot of pressure on him in that situation. I thought it was a bit unfair, but he went on to do well in the end.'

Ben said that his experiences of the 15-point season were both positive and negative, saying that despite being from a strong Newcastle United supporting area of the North East, he became attached to Sunderland.

'It was mixed emotions. Being at the club for so long, I'm from Newcastle way, but I was always at Sunderland; I got a lot of stick growing up for that. I was never a Sunderland fan, but when it becomes a place where I went almost every day for years, you become really attached.'

'It was mixed emotions really. Obviously for a young player, you want to play and better your career. At the same time, with what was happening at the club, it was tough. I was over the moon that I was in the team and playing, but it was a tough time and we were really struggling.'

Ben admitted that the reasons for Sunderland's struggle during that season came down simply to a lack of funding.

Like I say, I don't really get involved in the financial side, but I don't think Mick had the backing that other managers in the league had.

'I think the record signing that year was Jon Stead and about £1.5 million, which is madness really when you think about it. This was in the Premier League which, even then, had players moving around for a lot of money.

'I think Mick had a tough job, and it showed. I just don't think we had enough. It was tough, but it's just one of them things; it wasn't meant to be.'

When asked for a comparison between the two managers he played under at Sunderland, Roy Keane and Mick McCarthy, Ben felt he couldn't say a great deal on the latter.

'I couldn't really speak too much about Roy Keane, I wasn't there long enough to really say much. Obviously with Mick, I was there with him a while. I was involved at the club when he was there. He was brilliant, that's all I could say when people ask about Mick. He was different class.'

Ben said that training was hard, but enjoyable to the point that some players needed to be forced to leave the training ground.

'The term people use is firm but fair. He is the epitome of that saying. He would work us hard daily, but on the flip side we had such a laugh in training; we used to enjoy going in to train. In the end, he needed to start fining players because they were staying around for too long, just playing head tennis and being in the gym. It was a good environment to be in.'

On Roy Keane, Ben felt that he was perhaps unable to truly see what the Irishman did when he came to Sunderland.

He said, 'When Roy Keane came in, I was probably still too young to appreciate what he did. He came in and sorted things, he had his own ways. Looking at it now, I think if I was at a club and he came in I would have loved it.

'As it was, I was a young player and I didn't know what to make of it. Roy Keane got the job done and got the team promoted. They did very well.'

Keane joined Sunderland at the end of the summer of 2006. Earlier that year, Niall Quinn had taken over as chairman with his Drumaville consortium. It was a big period of change on Wearside, and Ben said it was an early lesson in how quickly things change in the world of professional football.

'It was a strange feeling. As you go on in your career, you kind of get used to it. Managers and players come and go, and you become accustomed to this. At the time when you're a young lad, it was a big change.

'Niall Quinn was very hands on, but it was very good. You could see which way they wanted to take the club, with Roy Keane and the staff they brought in. You could see there was a real buzz about the place, but I wasn't there quite long enough to remember it all. I just remember Keane coming in was unbelievable, the legend that he is.

'I remember that training was good. He came in and had his ways, the lads enjoyed training and it was a real breath of fresh air.'

Ben's last season at Sunderland started with him as the number-one keeper at the Stadium of Light. He explained how he felt he started the 2006-07 campaign.

'I think I started OK, maybe a bit hit and miss, but it's what would be expected from a young keeper. I didn't really have the experience; I was still young and maybe a bit delusional in my own head.'

He wished that things had worked out slightly differently, and he has passed on this advice to young goalkeepers he has come across since.

'Looking back, obviously you can't regret anything, but I've given advice to other keepers, including my brother, that you need to get out and play. I think that is something I should have done, at that age of 18 or 19, maybe a better plan for me would have been going out and getting 100 games at a League One or League Two team. This would be just to get the games in.

'As it was, I went straight into the firing line at a young age, with no real experience of men's football, to be honest. Like I say, I was enjoying it; I absolutely loved it. I had a mixed bag; I had some bad games and a few decent games. It was one of those things, you come to expect it from a young keeper who hasn't really played.'

In January 2006 Ben moved to Tottenham Hotspur after attracting attention from the London club. He decided that, at the age he was, it was a move he wanted to make, even though part of him wished he had stayed on Wearside for longer.

'Once I heard about the Tottenham move, I just felt at the time, when a club like that comes in for you, it was a move I couldn't turn down. Looking back, maybe the best option would have been to stay at Sunderland, but who knows. As an 18/19-year-old and you get a chance to join a club like that – it's quite hard to turn down.'

Ben said it was the mentality of his age that encouraged and convinced him to take up the offer and make the switch to White Hart Lane.

'I didn't so much want to go and test myself, it was more of having a young mentality. I talk to young keepers and young players at the time about their career. I had just signed a new contract, so it wasn't about the money.

'I had just had a bad game; I think it was Preston away. The whole team had a bad game, but I particularly had a poor game.'

The match Ben talks about was his last for Sunderland. In October 2006 Roy Keane's Sunderland visited Preston North End. The match was lost by half-time, with the hosts going in at the break 3-0 up thanks to goals from former Sunderland striker Danny Dichio, Graham Alexander and an own goal from Dean Whitehead. The match ended 4-1, with Simon Whaley bagging Preston's fourth and Stanislav Varga sealing a consolation goal for Sunderland.

Ben reflected on his mixed emotions surrounding the defeat at Deepdale and how he came to see Keane's decision as important.

'I remember the gaffer was going to put Wardy [Darren Ward] in and I was fuming at the time, but looking back it was absolutely the right decision. Wardy was an experienced, good goalkeeper and at the time was exactly what the team needed. I knew that I probably wasn't going to play much, even though I signed the new contract, I knew that I wasn't going to play for a while.'

'Then when I heard about the Tottenham move, it was quite flattering. Once I heard about it, I wanted to go. Looking back, whether it was the right decision remains to be seen.'

Ben spoke about his time at Tottenham, and how the changing of managers didn't help his efforts to become more involved at the club.

'It was tough to go to a club like Tottenham. What happened was I went when Martin Jol was there; he was a big fan of mine. He would talk to you and give you confidence, like if I stick with it, I could have a great chance of getting into the team.'

'It was difficult. Martin Jol got sacked and we brought in Juande Ramos, who for me I couldn't get away with. The training was different, and he brought in a different goalkeeping coach, then, all of a sudden, I found myself having to impress a new manager.'

He added that he had his work cut out due to the pedigree of goalkeeper that was at the club through his time there.

'But at the time I had England's number one ahead of me, a lot of the time I had really good goalkeepers around me. I had Paul Robinson, Radek Cerny, then Brad Friedel, Carlo Cudicini, Gomes. We had goalkeepers who are second choice whilst being international players who had played 100 times for their country.'

Ben said that if the nature of his loan moves were different it could have added to his confidence and ultimately benefited his career.

'It was tough, with a club like Tottenham there were so many good, experienced goalkeepers there. It was hard to break through. There were a lot of loan moves, but they were very hit and miss. At the time, I was in the same age bracket as Joe Hart.

'He went out on loan for a full season, where he would play 40 matches. He was at a few different clubs. It was the same as Pickers [Jordan Pickford] who went out to Bradford to get games in.

'With me, it would be a case of the season would start, I would be on the fringes of playing. I was always the second or third choice. I was basically told I couldn't go out on loan because I might be involved. The season starts, I wasn't involved, and I was thinking, "where do we go from here?"'

Ben's frustration was born out of never getting a full crack at regular first-team football during his time at Tottenham or out on loan.

'I'd go out on loan for a month or maybe three months, it was always very stop-start. I think one season I went on loan three times to try and get first-team football, and to not play in the reserves. It was very stop-start, I would go out and play a few games here and there and then go back to Tottenham and get assessed.'

One manager made Ben feel more involved with the squad, but it was a small consolation after the previous years.

'It wasn't until Harry Redknapp came in that I started being involved with the team. I was on the bench more, I played a few and I was travelling to a few of the European games. That's when I started feeling part of it. Apart from this, I never really felt part of it.'

He said that, looking back, his move to a Premier League side is something that he wouldn't do again.

'At Sunderland, I had been there so long, and I still talk to staff now who were there at the same time, I feel part of the family. At Tottenham, I didn't, and it was hard to get going.'

Ben was most recently at Bolton Wanderers, during a turbulent time for the club which resulted in the club being deducted points after relegation to League One.

He explained to some extent what happened at Bolton and how it was one of several factors that made him decide to take a break from playing.

'There was the stuff which happened at Bolton with players not getting paid, and I wanted to just take a step back. I had a few personal problems at home too. I had such a good time at Bolton, and, once everything started happening, Phil Parkinson got hung out to dry in the season we got relegated, I just wanted to take a step back after all of this.'

Ben reiterated that the break from football wouldn't be permanent, and that he feels he still has plenty to offer as a professional goalkeeper.

'I'm 33 years old, I still have a lot left in the tank and I'm just weighing up the options at the moment. I want to be as close to home as possible, but I'll take the time to look at it. If something pops up which is going to be right for me, I'll look at it. If not, I'll maybe move on to the next stage.'

Having thoroughly enjoyed his time at the club, Ben has plenty of good memories of Sunderland, one of the best being coming through the ranks and making it into the first team.

'I've spoken about it before, all the time I had at Sunderland was unbelievable. Being involved in the promotion season, it was brilliant. It was brilliant being at the club, it was so well run at the time. There were some great people at the club and to come through from such a young age, break through and to play at the Stadium of Light in front of the fans, it was great.'

The special bond Ben was a part of at Sunderland, from within the academy through to when he was part of the first-team dressing room, is something he has only come close to on one occasion since. He hopes it is something he can find again.

'It's a memory which I will cherish. The closest I've had to that feeling of camaraderie and work ethic was when I went to Bolton. We got promoted and then, the season after, we stay in the Championship whilst under an embargo and being unable to bring any players in and selling our best players; we were up against it.

'This was the closest feeling I had to being back at Sunderland. That kind of spirit is something that I have looked for. It was a brilliant time. I just hope the club can get back up to where it belongs.'

Ben Alnwick was an example of the kind of players Sunderland developed through their academy set up during the 2000s. He put the work in, represented the club in the top two divisions of English football, and departed Wearside to carry on a career as a reliable and consistent shot stopper.

STEVEN CALDWELL

Steven Caldwell is part of a unique club along with some other high-profile names who have played on Wearside. He is one of the very few players who crossed the great divide and played for both Sunderland and Newcastle.

Always an interesting talking point with supporters of both teams, Steven let his football do the talking whilst on Wearside. Making over 70 appearances in the top-two tiers for Sunderland, he quickly became a trustworthy centre-half.

Amongst his four goals in red-and-white stripes was the winner against Leicester City to seal Sunderland's return to the top tier of English football.

Steven started his professional career with his brother Gary at Newcastle in 1997. During his seven years on Tyneside, he had loan spells at Blackpool, Bradford and Leeds United. By 2007 injuries had seen Steven fall out of the set up at Sunderland and he went on to make over 100 appearances for Burnley.

A short spell at Wigan was followed by two years at Birmingham City. The next and final move of Steven's career saw him head across the Atlantic Ocean for two years at Toronto FC before hanging up his boots in 2015.

Yet before the Canadian days, Steven had a solid two seasons playing for Sunderland. Signing after being released by Newcastle, he quickly sparked a partnership with Republic of Ireland international Gary Breen during a campaign that would see the Black Cats crowned champions of the Championship. The pair made up a relatively settled back line, which other players in the squad would be hard pressed to break into.

Steven talked of what brought him to Sunderland and why he wanted to remain in the North East after leaving Newcastle.

'I loved playing football in the North East. Sunderland was a massive club to me, and I had a desire to work with Mick McCarthy.'

Mick McCarthy was the man to bring Steven to the Stadium of Light to start the process of building a team to get Sunderland back to the Premiership at the second attempt, and to move on from the heartache of a play-off semi-final defeat the previous season.

Steven said that it was somewhat of an experience to work with the man from Barnsley, as he learned things he kept in mind for the rest of his career.

'It was tough for me, especially at the start. Mick is a blunt man. He tells you how it is. Even more so to centre-halves! It took a while to get to know him and, in some ways, I think we are quite alike, so that caused conflict sometimes.

'In the end, he's a man I admire greatly. The things I learnt from him cannot be overstated. I am very grateful to have worked with him.'

Whatever Steven thought of his relationship with McCarthy, there was respect enough for the centre-half to be named as his vice-captain alongside skipper Gary Breen.

Mick McCarthy is a manager who, despite being at the club during two of the most disappointing seasons in Sunderland's history, is fondly remembered by many fans. His straight-talking, no-nonsense attitude seemed fitting for a team not flush with talent but ripe with honesty.

Steven's relationship with McCarthy strengthened during the highs and lows of his career at Sunderland. His first season at the Stadium of Light was one of the more successful in Sunderland's recent history. A total of 29 wins and 94 points saw the club crowned champions with games to spare, finishing seven points clear of second-placed Wigan Athletic.

Steven, who was vice-captain for the campaign, found the back of the net four times, including the winner against Leicester in April to seal promotion back to the big time.

When asked about why he thought the season was a success, Steven focussed his answer around a good team morale.

'The key to success was team spirit. Togetherness. An accountability to each other that encouraged honesty and ruthlessness. It wasn't for the faint hearted! But it was very, very special.'

Steven said that his experience in the 2004-05 campaign was one of the best of his career, and a side that he had good memories from. He admitted the squad wasn't saturated in talent but made up for it in other departments.

'Yes. It was certainly one of the most memorable. Not the most talented. Just good, honest people demanding more from each other. A great social group and we knew how to have fun.

'At the end of the 2004/05 Championship season we were the best team by far, and if it kept going we would have moved further and further clear from the rest.'

Steven was a man who put the icing on the cake in a very successful campaign for Mick McCarthy's Sunderland. His winner in a 2-1 win over Leicester City confirmed a promotion which had looked nailed-on for most of the season.

Ever the professional, Steven had only one thought after scoring one of the most pivotal goals of his career. It was a case of bag the vital goal and then get back to do the day job for the Scottish international.

When asked what his first thought was after scoring the goal, he said, 'Get back and defend! It wasn't one of our best performances. But we were gritty. We had resilience. That was probably our greatest strength.

'After the game we were ecstatic of course. Then the magnitude of scoring that goal sunk in and ever since I have been very proud to have scored it.'

Promotion to the Premier League for the 2005-06 campaign was a great success for the club, but their preparations were dealt a blow with the sale of their top scorer in the summer. Marcus Stewart found the back of the net 17 times in all competitions during the campaign, showing an instinct which could have proved useful in the Premier League.

Steven said that Sunderland did not just lose a goalscorer, but also a personality from within the squad.

When asked if it was concerning to see Stewart depart during the summer, he said, 'Not concern as such. We knew it was going to be difficult. The Premier League is a different beast. We had to try and keep that togetherness while adding quality.

'We were losing a goalscorer in Stewy and a very important character in the changing room. He was never going to be easy to replace.'

During the highs of the 2004-05 promotion from the Championship and lows of the 2005-06 Premier League season, Steven was partnered at centre-back with Republic of Ireland international Gary Breen. The pair played together during two very different campaigns for Sunderland, and Steven had plenty of praise for his former team-mate.

He said, 'It was great. We complimented each other well. I had a lot of respect for [Gary] and he was a terrific player.'

The build-up to a season in the Premier League would, for many clubs, be the same as any other season. For Sunderland, there were wholesale changes including the departure of their top scorer from the previous campaign.

Sunderland brought in 14 new faces over the course of the season, with 17 departing either permanently or on loan as the campaign progressed. The overturn at the club could have been the reason behind the team's poor season, or that many of the players brought in by Mick McCarthy were not cut out for life at the top level of English football.

Sunderland began the campaign with many players who had little or no Premier League experience, something which would prove to be decisive as the season wore on.

Steven was one of the players within the squad to have had top-flight experience, first with Newcastle United and later whilst on loan at Leeds United. He played in both the last game in the Championship against Stoke City and Sunderland's opening Premier League fixture against Charlton Athletic.

This fixture ended in a 3-1 defeat for the Black Cats, the first of 29 losses during a hugely disappointing season.

Despite the way the season played out, Steven said that there was the usual pre-season optimism before a ball had been kicked.

When asked if there was any concern ahead of the new campaign, Steven said, 'Not really. We wanted to get started. We felt like we could do well once we figured it out. It all sort of hit home for me when we played Charlton on the first weekend. This was a game we obviously felt we could win.

'We lost quite comfortably and I think we all knew that the quality of opposition was going to be way stronger on a weekly basis. Momentum was everything with that team and we just couldn't get anything going that season.

'Matters off the pitch and behind the scenes are always a concern to supporters. Sunderland have had their fair share of this in recent years in terms of change of ownership. That wasn't my concern. I was paid to be a player. I focussed on that. I think that it's easy to attach blame in this game and I tried my best to stay clear of that.'

The Stadium of Light quickly became a place of doom and gloom as week in, week out visiting sides left with the points. Sunderland won just one home game throughout the season; this came in their final home match of the season against Fulham.

Despite the woeful home record, Sunderland fans still came in their numbers to follow their side, with an average home attendance of almost 34,000 throughout the campaign. They would only be rewarded on their final trip to the Stadium of Light that season.

The one win on home soil came in bizarre circumstances, with the original fixture in April 2006 being abandoned with the Black Cats 1-0 down.

Steven said that playing in a tough environment such as the Stadium of Light was a test for the players in the 2005-06 season but that the squad never gave up when on the pitch.

He said, 'It wasn't easy for anybody. I've always said the North East can be the best and the worst places in the world to play football. There is nowhere to hide and it'd be more intense than anywhere I have ever played. We never gave up. We kept fighting; however, confidence was low and results didn't come.'

Steve is one of the few players who has experienced the passionate but often hostile arenas of two North East clubs. He embraced it, many players before and after him have crumbled in front of these crowds.

The influx of new players and many squad members underperforming were, for Steven, key factors in the club's failure to adjust to life in the Premier League.

He said, 'I think people under-performed. I think too many new faces came in. I think money would have been better spent on two or three players of real quality. In the end, that spirit was lost, and we realised what a part it played in our success.'

In March 2006, having won just two of 28 matches, Mick McCarthy was sacked as Sunderland manager. Coach Kevin Ball was given the reigns until the end of the season. Exactly what you would expect. Fight, desire, passion.

Steven had a mixed bag of a Sunderland career. He went from being part of a squad that romped to the Championship title with over 90 points one season, to finishing rock bottom of the Premier League with 15 points the next. Yet he loved his time on Wearside, and looking out for the results of Sunderland matches is still something he does; even from a different continent.

He said, 'I'm proud to have worn the shirt. It's still one of the first results I look for. I hope the fans appreciate that I gave my all. It's a very special football club because of the people who love it.

'I played two and a half seasons. The first one we won the Championship. The second was disappointing. I also feel we were a little unlucky. We didn't get hammered much that season. We were often so near yet so far. The last half season the club went on to be promoted again. All in all, I think we achieved a decent amount.'

It is interesting and important that Steven points out the fact that despite losing so many matches in the 2005-06 season, Sunderland were rarely beaten heavily. In fact, 15 of the clubs 29 defeats were by a single-goal margin. Some would argue that this is null and void considering how many times Sunderland chalked up defeat, but it is the thinnest of silver linings in a forgettable campaign for the Black Cats.

After leaving the Stadium of Light, Steven turned out for Burnley, Wigan Athletic and Birmingham City before finishing his playing career across the Atlantic in Canada. The North American country is where Steven now plies his trade.

On his Canadian adventure so far, he said, 'I finished my career with Toronto FC of MLS. I now broadcast on Canadian TV and I'm an assistant coach for the Canadian men's national team.'

It was clear that Steven thoroughly enjoyed his time on Wearside. Few players have been at the club through the highs of a promotion and the lows of a (then) record-breaking lowest points total in the top flight.

Steven put his feelings about playing for Sunderland in one clear sentence. His solid performances made sure that he will be remembered by supporters as someone who always put a shift in.

He said, 'It was a pleasure and a privilege to represent the shirt.'

His third season on Wearside may have been restricted to just 11 appearances, but it was the way he had stepped up in the previous two seasons which will make Steven a respected player at Sunderland.

His two full campaigns were total opposites, but many players would have crumbled during a season half as devastating as 2005-06 was for Sunderland. Steven Caldwell was present through some of the highest highs as well as the lowest of the lows seen at Sunderland in the 21st century, and he seems to have enjoyed almost all of it.

DANNY COLLINS

Danny Collins is from a category of Sunderland players who have played a part in more successful campaigns in the last 20 years than those which ended in disappointment. On top of being one of these players, he is one who worked hard and showed he wanted to be in a red and white shirt on Wearside – the kind of player who is seen less and less at Sunderland.

The Welshman was signed from Chester City after playing the first dozen matches at the newly promoted League Two club. A central-defender who was also utilised at full-back, Danny came to Sunderland with a lot of promise. He would leave as one of the more memorable players to be at the club in the 21st century.

His time at the club lasted six years, coming to an end in 2009 as Danny moved to Stoke City. For the Potters, Danny played 60 times in a two-year period. the majority of the 2011-12 season was made up in loan moves, firstly at Ipswich Town and then West Ham United. His next permanent move was to Nottingham Forest for the start of the 2012-13 season. Almost 80 matches and one goal later for Forest, and Danny was on the move again. This time to South Yorkshire and Rotherham United. Danny spent one season at the New York Stadium, appearing 24 times for the Championship side.

From 2016 to 2019, Danny played for Grimsby Town, appearing over 100 times for the Mariners. It was here he played his last football, although he explained that there has been no official retirement statement yet.

Danny had made over 70 appearances for Chester City when he signed for Sunderland. The year before moving to the Stadium of Light, he made 45 appearances and scored twice as Chester won the Conference title, losing just four matches in the process.

He spoke about his move to Sunderland, when other teams were interested in his signature, and how he was in the North East just a day after playing his last match for Chester.

'I was at Chester at the time and progressing there. We'd just been promoted back to the Football League from the conference and I think I'd played 10/12 games at the start of that season. I knew there was a bit of interest from a few clubs, Sunderland being one.

'I played a game for Chester on the Saturday then on the evening my agent rang me to say Sunderland had agreed a deal with Chester. Basically, I had to then get my stuff packed ready to move up to Sunderland on the Sunday.'

Danny was aware that teams higher up in the English footballing pyramid were interested, and the wheels were very soon in motion for his move to Sunderland.

'I knew there was interest in me, I think Sheffield United and Everton as well as Sunderland. When my agent called me, I can't remember off the top of my head, but he basically said I would be going up for a medical on the Sunday.'

The change in situation and setting was something that amazed Danny. Few players have gone from League Two to the Championship in a matter of hours, and even less would have done this move firstly at Danny's age and secondly to a team with a ground the size of Sunderland's.

'I was astonished. The size of the club and everything compared to what I was used to daily at Chester. The surroundings, the training ground, the stadium, just everything really. Sunderland were sat fourth in the championship at the time I think, so it was a major step up in what I was used to.'

Danny signed at a point when Sunderland had a settled back four as they prepped to get back to the Premier League. He acknowledged that he needed to work hard for a place in the team, and this helped him to make over a dozen appearances as Sunderland won the league.

'The back four at that point were George McCartney, Gary Breen, Steven Caldwell and Stephen Wright. Neil Collins had not long signed and he was in the same boat as me, still young. We had to bide our time with the team playing well. I think I played about 12 games in that first promotion season, so it was a good experience.'

Danny's first full season as a Sunderland player was perhaps the most forgettable of the 21st century so far for supporters. The club finished bottom of the Premier League with just 15 points, registering just three wins.

He said that the campaign was one which brought the mood down across the club, and that the fans let the players know they weren't happy. Danny admitted that it was good to get away from football for a short period before kicking off again in the Championship.

'It was a disappointing season; we'd gone down a few games before the end of the season, on the points tally especially. The stadium, the fans and everybody sort of lets you know about it. It was a case of getting away from it in the summer, stew over it for a couple of weeks and then get ready to go in again at pre-season to try and put it right.'

Danny added that, when back in the Championship, it took a while to get the club moving in the right direction again, but the work soon paid off once new manager Roy Keane was appointed.

'The aim was to hit the ground running, which of course we didn't at first, but things changed after Roy came in and we got back to winning ways.'

Danny said that the relegation from the Premier League gave himself and everyone at the club plenty to think about.

'No one wants to get relegated. It affects the fans and the workforce in and around the ground. People lose jobs and wages are cut. You go away on holiday but you're still thinking about it. We dropped down into the Championship and it was a lot to mull over.

'If everyone comes in and is still gloomy then it's not a good start to the season, so you need to put it behind you as quick as you can once we're in to get ready, go again, and try and get it right.'

Danny played most of his football at Sunderland under two managers. Mick McCarthy and Roy Keane have a chequered history together from their involvement with the Republic of Ireland at the 2002 World Cup. As well as this, both lead Sunderland for several years and oversaw league titles

Danny was a big part of both, and he was hugely deserving of both league winner's medals.

Talking about his former managers, Danny started with the man who brought him to the Stadium of Light in the first place.

He said, 'Mick is honest, you get what you see with him. All his interviews he tells it how it is. He's honest with the lads and he gets stuck into players at half-time and at the training ground when things weren't going to plan. I enjoyed working with him.

'It was the same thing with Roy. They were both hands on, maybe Mick more than Roy. Both were demanding of the players; they knew what they wanted and expected out of the team. If lads weren't doing it, both would let them know about it. When Roy came, he brought a lot of new players in. We'd had a bad start to the season under Quinny.'

There was a major shake-up at Sunderland during the summer and early weeks of the 2006-07 season, with Danny feeling it was vital the new players gelled quickly. After four straight defeats, as well as a humiliating League Cup defeat away to Bury, things needed to change, and fast.

'It could have gone either way, when a team brings in a load of new players it sometimes takes time for them to bond. Thankfully for us, it happened quickly, and we went on a good run and got ourselves up the other end of the table.'

Danny talked about the 15-point season in detail. It was his first opportunity to play Premier League football and he suggested it was why he felt the team struggled. He wasn't the only player from this period to suggest Mick McCarthy had his hands tied financially well before a ball was kicked.

'When we went up the first time, it was always going to be tough as I don't think Mick had too much to spend. We had a low budget compared to other sides at the time. Others and I hadn't played in the Premier League before, so it was a big learning curve.'

Sunderland were often not beaten heavily, but they did lose consistently throughout the season. 29 defeats are 29 defeats, it doesn't matter how you look at them. However, Danny felt it acted as a lesson for the following seasons and for Sunderland's next, more successful, campaign in the Premier League.

'You need to hit the ground running. During that season we didn't take too many hidings, we lost 1-0 and 2-1 quite a lot. It was a frustrating season. We went down with 15 points, but it made us stronger in terms of the season after and for when we came back into the Premier League.'

Under Roy Keane, Sunderland were strengthened as a defensive unit. The infamous 15-point season saw the Black Cats ship 69 goals in 38 league matches. This meant that the issue needed to be sorted if Sunderland were to make an immediate return to the Premier League.

One signing during the season was a 19-year-old Jonny Evans who joined on loan in the January transfer window. Along with Evans and Nyron Nosworthy, who was also signed by Mick McCarthy, Danny was one of a solid trio of central-defender options for Sunderland. This was also the case in the 2007-08 campaign when, again, Evans joined on loan from Manchester United. Danny spoke of his old team-mates, firstly Nosworthy and then Evans.

'Nyron is a good lad, he's quite relaxed. In football you get all kinds of characters. Some lads are quiet, and others are boisterous all around the training ground. Nugsy is quite a quiet lad but he does like a laugh.

'Like with Jonny, I could always have a laugh and a joke with him. It helps when you're winning games. When you're struggling, you tend to find out who the real characters are. That season under Roy we were on a good run and the place was upbeat. It was a good place to be.'

Danny's second season in the Premier League saw him feature in 36 of Sunderland's 38 league games. A regular solid performer, Danny also found the net in a 3-1 win at Fulham in April 2008. He should have opened his account much earlier in the season, however, when Aston Villa were in town in December 2007.

The match was finely poised at 1-1. Danny Higginbotham had given Sunderland a first-half lead before Shaun Maloney curled in a free kick late in the second half. The Black Cats thought they had their winner in stoppage time; however, it wasn't to be.

Danny explained how it felt to have a goal that few could see any fault with disallowed so late in the game.

'I remember it well. I think it was the 92nd minute and we got a corner. I got a good run and jump on Scott Carson; he's come out to punch it and I got a clean head on it and scored. I've seen it go in, ran off celebrating and then five seconds later I turn around and see Steve Bennett has disallowed it. I went from a feeling up there to disappointment in seconds. It was a real rollercoaster of emotions.'

Sunderland formed a good habit of scoring late goals in both this season and the previous campaign, yet this was one occasion where there wouldn't be last-gasp jubilation at the Stadium of Light.

The 2008-09 campaign again saw Danny feature heavily, playing 41 times in league and cup as well as being named player of the season.

During this season, Roy Keane departed Sunderland after over two years in charge. He was the last manager to take charge of Sunderland in 100 matches. Keane was also the last Sunderland manager to win silverware at the club, which is now 13 years and counting. Getting Sunderland promoted and then stable in the top flight is something that feels a long time from being repeated, especially in the current climate.

Keane's tenure at the club came after a 4-1 home defeat to Bolton Wanderers, in a match where Sunderland took the lead through Djibril Cisse

Danny said that Keane's departure was a surprise at first, but as more information came out about why the Irishman left Wearside, the more it made sense.

'It was a surprise. It came out later that he wasn't too happy with the board and stuff like that. I don't think I expected it to come so soon. I think we played Bolton on the Saturday and he was gone soon after that. It's the type of person he is, he wasn't happy with things, so he called it a day and stepped down.'

For Danny, the move to Sunderland was a significant step up personally as well as professionally. Having played his youth football in North Wales, the north of England was a very different change of scenery.

'It was my first move away from home to play. I'd lived in north Wales all my life, obviously playing for Chester. It was a ten-minute drive from where I lived, up until I was 24 when I signed for Sunderland.

'It's a three-hour drive to where I lived, so it was the first time I'd ventured away from home. I settled in pretty quick to be fair; there were a few lads who had also joined at the same time who were in the same situation as me. I was made welcome by the lads at the club which did help as well.'

For many supporters, Danny was a constant professional and a player who was much admired throughout his time at the club. The man himself seemed to love the club as much as people at the club admired him.

'From the minute I got up here I started enjoying it. working under Mick and seeing the facilities made it easier. As a player you want to play in big stadiums and have good training grounds to work in every day.'

Danny has played over 500 times in the professional game but suggested that he isn't quite finished on the pitch yet. He also gave an idea of what else he wants to do in the game once he knows his playing days are done.

'I haven't officially said I have retired yet, just in case I want to throw the boots back on, but I finished at Grimsby last year and I was away in the summer assessing things. Currently I have done a bit of stuff with Sunderland and the media, so I would look to do some more of that. I have done some coaching as well; I'd look to get into more of this and to put something back into the game.'

The coaching is an option that Danny has kept open to prevent him from needing to miss the game which he has been involved in most of his life.

'I think I would miss not being on the pitch after playing for the last 19 years. It's something I have enjoyed all my life and I think I can pass on the experience I have gained.

'Now, I am edging towards retirement and just looking at the next steps which is, for me, the media and coaching side of the game.'

As an ending statement, Danny summed up his time at Sunderland and, despite the unpredictability which came with the club, that he cherished the times he played.

'From the minute I came in to the minute I left, obviously we had ups and downs, I loved every moment. I enjoyed it most out of my career, my family is from up here now and I am just enjoying it. we've settled in the area and everything about the club is great.'

Danny added that he struggles to see why so many players fail to appreciate their time at Sunderland, suggesting that for too many their time playing for the club is only realised once they have departed Wearside.

He fell in love with the club, and still hopes the club does well as much as some supporters. The idea that players found it hard work to play for Sunderland is something which isn't shared by Danny.

'You take to the club; other players should enjoy being up here more. Some players find it a chore, which I just can't understand. A lot of players won't realise until after they have left the club what they had.'

Danny Collins is a player who understood the club when he was still there, and what he says is perhaps more truthful than many other professional footballers would care to believe. Sunderland is a football club that has gotten under the skin of many players in the past and, hopefully, will continue to do so in the future.

Danny isn't the first player to fall in love with the club, but he was one who will always be fondly remembered on Wearside for putting in the graft that Sunderland supporters crave from their team. He was a player who got the job done and was deservedly associated with some of the better seasons for Sunderland in the 21st century.

JUSTIN HOYTE

Justin Hoyte was born in Leytonstone, East London, in November 1984. An Arsenal fan from a young age, Justin joined the Gunners at the age of nine. He developed through the club's academy and in July 2002 he signed as a professional.

In a six-year period at Highbury, and from 2006 the Emirates Stadium, Justin made almost 70 appearances. He found the back of the net in a 4-0 win over Charlton Athletic in January 2007, which made him the first English goalscorer for Arsenal at their new home.

A permanent move away from North London was speculated, but it was a loan move to newly promoted Sunderland for the start of the 2005-06 campaign which got Justin's career on the move. In league and cup, Justin played 30 times for the Black Cats, scoring in a 4-1 home defeat to Newcastle United in April 2006. In what was a poor season for Sunderland, Justin gained a lot of experience of being at the wrong end of the Premier League table – experience that he would never have faced at Arsenal.

Justin went back to Arsenal, playing 22 times in the Premier League in the 2006-07 season. The first permanent move of his career took him to a town just to the south of Sunderland. Between 2008 and 2014, he made over 160 appearances for Middlesbrough. Although his first season on Teesside ended in relegation from the Premier League, Justin would become a regular during several seasons in the Championship.

A short spell at Millwall followed before Justin moved across to Essex to spend the 2015-16 season at Dagenham & Redbridge. He played 28 times for the League Two side, before moving across the Atlantic Ocean to ply his trade stateside.

At the start of the 2017 United States League Championship, the second tier of football in America, Justin joined FC Cincinnati. Within three seasons, he made himself a regular and his side became reached the MLS for the first time in 2018. He is currently playing in Florida for newly formed Miami Beach Club de Futbol. This side came into existence in 2019, and Justin has big plans for his latest club.

Going back to when he first found out Sunderland were interested in his signature, Justin spoke of how it was a perfect opportunity and one which he couldn't wait to get started on.

'It was the opportunity to play regular football. When Mick McCarthy, who was manager at the time, showed interest in taking me on loan when I'd only been playing one or two games at Arsenal. It was a chance to go to a big and well-followed side in Sunderland.

'When I thought of what that would do for me gaining experience, I saw it as a great opportunity to further my career by playing Premier League matches.'

Justin's early years at Arsenal saw him playing and training alongside some of the best players ever to play for the Gunners. As a fan of the club, he explained how it was a dream come true to share a dressing room with his heroes.

'It was amazing. Firstly I was an Arsenal supporter from a young age so to be able to even sit in the same dressing room as some of these players who I regarded as Arsenal greats, who I looked up to and watched on TV, and getting to train with them on a daily basis and then sitting down as part of the same squad, getting on the pitch and playing alongside them, was a dream come true.

'I am grateful for this. To go from being a fan, running after the team bus after they had won things, to then being a part of the team was fantastic. I learned so much playing and training alongside these players.'

Justin said that it was incredible to be part of a squad that has gone down in footballing history as one of the best to grace the Premier League, and he picked out two of these players as the ones who stood out for him in his early years.

'It was the same with everyone. They were top, world-class players from all over the world. I learned from them and their experiences and saw what they had accomplished as players. I took little bits from different people, I was coming through the youth team into the first team, and Ashley Cole took me under his wing a bit.

'Then there was Patrick Viera, who was a real leader for the team. I've taken that into my career and base it on how he was with people around the training pitch and the stadium.'

In the summer of 2005, Justin was 20 and ready to play regular first-team football. Despite interest from Ipswich Town, Justin's manager Arsene Wenger wanted the fullback to play Premier League football. It is here that Sunderland began to show interest in Justin's signature. He spoke of how the season at the Stadium of Light came at an ideal point in his career.

'For me, it was a perfect time. Just for the fact that I was trying to knock on the door of the first team at Arsenal. Getting that regular, Premier League, first-team football at Sunderland and growing up into my own person, living away from home and all of this really helped my later career and me getting more matches for Arsenal.

'If I didn't have that opportunity to go on loan to Sunderland, I might not have been able to play the matches I did for Arsenal. I feel that the time at Sunderland really did help get my career started.'

Going back to his first manager, Justin talked highly of Wenger as a man and a manager. He could see Justin being out on loan and gaining vital experience.

On his relationship with Arsene Wenger, Justin said, 'It was really good. At the time when Sunderland were interested, we spoke about the possibility of going on loan to a team like Sunderland. He always spoke to me in pre-season and in training and after games.'

Justin added that his manager recommended the move to Sunderland as it would provide a good test for him.

'He told me that Sunderland would be a great opportunity to play regular football, something different to what it's like at Arsenal. He thought I could learn and develop more as a player by going out on loan. We had a good relationship in the sense of one between a manager and a player.'

According to Justin, Arsene Wenger made it clear that he would only let him leave if it was on loan to another Premier League side. It would be a move that would give Justin the breakthrough top-flight season both he and his manager wanted for him.

'Yes, he sort of did. Obviously, I wanted to get a break into the Arsenal team which meant getting into a Premier League team. Sunderland were probably the first team to come in for me, so in that sense it was a perfect place for me to learn and develop, a perfect place to play within the Premier League and another chance to establish myself as a Premier League player.'

The Black Cats were the first and, as far as Justin was aware, the only side to come in for him during the summer. The move was helped by a Sunderland first-team regular picking up an injury, meaning that the right-back position was vacant at the Stadium of Light.

'It was just Sunderland, literally the first team, which came in for me. The defender at the time, I think it was Stephen Wright, had picked up an injury and I was the next one they called. In that sense I think Sunderland were the first team, I'm not sure if there was any other side at the time because I was focussed on playing for Arsenal.

'As soon as I heard that Sunderland were interested, I was told by Arsene Wenger and my agent that I would be going up there, and I jumped at the opportunity. I was up for the challenge and I was willing to drive and move up north and get started.'

Justin's season on Wearside was a mixed bag. He was a regular in the side, but it was a side that accumulated just 15 points throughout the season. The people at the club made the transition from London to Sunderland far easier for him.

'For me, it was fantastic. I always tell everyone that the season we had was so disappointing in the way we got relegated, but I really enjoyed my time up there.

This was the case both on and off the field, the players I was playing around and the facilities, the coaching staff and everyone who was there at the time were great.

'I felt like we all had a really good relationship. They were very welcoming and for me, as someone who travelled up north for the first time and leaving London; to go to a place like Sunderland it could be daunting. Yet for me it was a move which I thoroughly enjoyed, and I was made to feel welcome as soon as I walked through the door.'

Going from London up to the North East alone could be daunting for anyone and there was always the chance that Justin would be unable to settle. However, he felt he fit in well with the layout of how things worked at Sunderland. He added he was helped to settle into the area by a man who would go down as a cult hero on Wearside and who had trodden the same London-to-Sunderland path as Justin earlier in that summer.

The different living conditions and being further away from family than ever before was challenging for Justin.

'It was different. I was born and raised in London; I had lived there all my life. To leave your home town and be somewhere you had never lived before, by yourself and without your family being nearby, was tough at first. But I feel I had someone at the club who helped me enormously in Nyron Nosworthy.

'He was from London and had moved up to Sunderland there just before I did. I think he was a perfect role model who helped me to settle into the team perfectly and into the city as well, so a lot of my thanks goes to him.'

The importance of Nosworthy's role in helping him settle in was not lost on Justin, as he added that things would have been far more difficult for him if it wasn't for the support of his fellow Londoner.

'If it wasn't for Nyron, some things would have been more difficult but at the same time it was an easy transition and one which I looked forward to. He is a great guy. I enjoyed the challenge and the experience of going up and playing for Sunderland and playing for such a well-supported team.'

Maintaining morale in a campaign where nothing went right may seem like an impossible task. For Sunderland fans, the 2005-06 Premier League season is one of those years. As a supporter in the stand, it was hard to see where the positivity could come from in a season of just three league wins from 38 matches.

However, Justin gave a lot of credit to the coaching staff and his team-mates at Sunderland for what they did to keep each other motivated.

'If I am honest, every player, and staff as well, did a great job of keeping the spirit up. I give a lot of credit to Mick McCarthy for what he did to keep the players going through the situation we found ourselves in. He kept the players motivated and kept them fighting until the end, regardless of what was going on with the club.

'Even when it was announced we had been relegated, the mood was disappointing but also positive in that we had our own careers to fight for as well as the fans who came to watch us every week.'

Despite not performing enough to stave off relegation, Justin saw every player in the squad as someone who brought something to the table.

'In that sense, I feel that every player was fighting for themselves, the club and the fans. With every player, their mood was down at times, but I think every player brought something to the group with their own personality. They kept the group together and kept us positive even though the situation at the time wasn't the best.'

Justin was brought into the club by Mick McCarthy ahead of the 2005-06 season. He spoke of what McCarthy was like to work with as a manager.

'It was great, I couldn't think of a better manager who could have brought me into a club at that time. From leaving Arsenal to then going to Sunderland, I couldn't have asked for a better manager to learn from. He was fantastic, it was a credit to be brought in by him.

'The day-to-day relationship was great. You could go to him about anything and he told you how it was and spoke the truth. He didn't hold back, which at that point in my career I needed. It was perfect.'

Justin's first two managers as a professional footballer were experienced in their roles even in 2005. Arsene Wenger first signed him up as a professional player and then Mick McCarthy gave Justin his first regular run of first-team games.

When asked about any differences between the management styles of his first two managers in the game, Justin said, 'Their management style was similar, just how they approached certain situations was different. Their attitude to certain circumstances differed. Mick McCarthy handles things differently to Arsene Wenger, but for me it was great to see two different sides of how to be a manager in certain situations.'

Justin found the back of the net once during his time on Wearside, and he couldn't have picked a bigger match to do so. Scoring in a Wear Tyne derby is something that will always make you remembered at Sunderland, even if the match in which Justin scored ended in a 4-1 victory for Newcastle.

Justin set up the move for his goal, playing the ball out wide to Jon Stead before running into the penalty area and slotting home past Shay Given. Sunderland held their own into the second half, but the defensive frailties which plagued them throughout the season once again crept into the side. Goals from Michael Chopra,

Alan Shearer, Charles N'Zogbia and Albert Luque gave the Magpies a comfortable victory

Talking through how it felt to score in a prestigious fixture to those in the North East, Justin said everything about it was fantastic.

'For me, it was a great moment. On a personal note, I don't score many goals, but to score in such a huge match was unbelievable. The celebration, the lead up to the goal, just scoring against your arch-rivals at the Stadium of Light was fantastic. For me, going on loan, it was one of the best achievements to score in such a huge game.

'That moment will always stay with me. When I retire, I can look back on that as a great achievement. OK, the result didn't go according to plan but personally you need to look on the bright side sometimes. It was a wonderful moment for myself and I was able to share that 10/20-minute period of joy with the Sunderland fans before I left the club.

'It was a great moment to share with not just my team-mates but also the fans, to score in such a big derby match.'

In this season, Sunderland's relegation was confirmed after a 0-0 draw away to Manchester United; it was ironically perhaps Sunderland's best defensive performance all season. This meant that the Black Cats had five matches in which they had nothing to play for but pride. Justin said that he noticed a change in the mentality of the players in these games, one of which was the defeat to Newcastle which he scored in.

'I think players had a bit more freedom, in the way that there was nothing to lose. We'd been relegated, even if we lost games it wouldn't make things any worse. I feel like a lot of players had that freedom and that there would be things to gain personally and as a team. We wanted to end on a high, win as many games as possible and finish on a high.

'You never know where it could lead to. In that sense, the players had more freedom and could express themselves after relegation was confirmed. They could play without any freedom purely because we had already been relegated, which wasn't a good time, but it gave us the chance to make the end of the season better than the rest of the campaign.'

The season in which Justin was a Sunderland player is not one which is looked upon fondly by locals. He said that the reasons behind the Black Cats nightmare season were simple:

'I just didn't think we were good enough for the Premier League that season. We didn't win enough matches and we didn't perform the way we should have. We lost a lot of games and conceded a lot of goals. Not performing well and conceding a lot of goals will ultimately lead to relegation. I think it was several things, but I don't blame anyone.

'We were a team, we tried to do our best every week and throughout training, we just didn't get the right results. Unfortunately, it ended in relegation.'

After enjoying two seasons in and around the first team at Arsenal, Justin made his first permanent move. This took him from London up to Teesside and to Gareth Southgate's Middlesbrough. He represented Boro in both the Premier League and the Championship, and it was a move made easier by already having familiar faces in the North East, according to Justin.

'I enjoyed my time there. Because of how well I settled into the area when I was at Sunderland, I was quite excited when I found out I was going back up to the north east to Middlesbrough. Through playing at Sunderland, I knew what the fans are like in the North East and I was looking forward to that again even if it was Middlesbrough this time.

'I was excited to get back up north and being a player in that part of the world again. It wasn't Sunderland, obviously, but it was great to be back up there. I lived close to Sunderland anyway, even when I was at Middlesbrough.'

As well as playing seven seasons in the north east of England, Justin turned out 18 times for Trinidad & Tobago later in his career, between 2013 and 2016. He is not the only Sunderland player in the last few decades to represent Trinidad, with Kenwyne Jones, Dwight Yorke, Stern John and Carlos Edwards also playing for the Soca Warriors before, during and after their time on Wearside.

Justin spoke about his experiences of travelling around the world to represent the Caribbean nation. He said, 'Playing international football has been amazing. I wish I had gone to Trinidad before I did. It was great at the time. I remember the coach at the time called up the players in England and called us into the squad. We had a great team and a great manager. We did well.

'For me, it was great to play at that level against some top players. You test yourself against the best players in the world for their country. I was also able to see more of the world, which was great too. To get the chance to play against the likes of Mexico and Argentina and in World Cup qualifiers, you can't get any higher than that as a professional player unless you reach the World Cup itself. It was great to be a part of the Trinidad national team.'

Justin now plays his football in the USA and has done for three years. In this time, he has already represented two sides, with the latter being one of the newest editions to the American game.

He talked of where he began in America and where it has taken him so far.

'I spent three years at Cincinnati and moved with them into the MLS and I'm now with a club called Miami Beach Club de Football, which is a new team that has started in the lower leagues. Hopefully, we will be in the USL divisions within the next year.'

The MLS and American football in general were once viewed as a chance for big-time European players to finish their careers in a nicer climate, but recent years has seen a significant rise in the quality of football in the USA. Justin feels that there are big differences between the sport in England and America, with the most noticeable being travelling.

'I would say the biggest difference is the travel. In England, the travel is usually a bus, train or a short flight to get to an away match. Over here, it could be anything from a two-hour flight up to a five-hour flight to game. I would say the travel is a huge difference.

'Another one would be the turf. In England, all you know are grass pitches, but in America there are a lot of AstroTurf pitches. This takes some getting used to, but the team I was at had a European feel to it. We would get crowds of around 25,000, so in that sense it was great to be a part of that set up because it felt like I was back home in that familiar setting and that size of a fan base.'

A further difference, according to Justin, is the intensity going into each match. This is down to the difference in the structure of the football pyramid in America to that of England.

'I think the day-to-day training, preparation and build-up to match day is completely different in America than compared to England. Playing in America now, I think it is more relaxed and stress-free than England. That's only because there is no relegation or promotion. This makes it perfect for me, in the latter stages of my career, to play here.'

Justin spoke more of what it's like to play in a division without an outright league champion and relegation places, saying that any side who reaches the play-off has had an excellent campaign.

'It's crazy. When I first got here I thought, "Well you obviously want to win the league," but here if you win the league that doesn't mean the season is over. There is a play-off and making it to the play-offs is a huge achievement for every team who gets there.

'We won the league as a team the next year and we were celebrating because we had come out on top and were champions, but because we didn't win the whole tournament when we played in the play-offs it was a disappointing season. Really, it should have been a huge achievement because we had technically won the league.

'It is crazy. We're looking around at other teams' results, but also we aren't. You try to focus on how your team is doing and making sure you make the play-offs. If you make the play-offs in America, it is a huge achievement. That's why everyone tries to get there.'

Going back to his time at Sunderland, Justin compared it to the other places he has played football. He appreciated the education he received at Wearside.

'It was a great starting point for me. It paved my way to playing more matches and enabled me to establish myself as a player in the top divisions of English football. If it wasn't for my time at Sunderland and what I learnt as a player, both on and off the field, my path in football would have been a lot different.

'I enjoyed every part of it, I'm pleased I went to Sunderland. It was a disappointment that we were relegated when I was there, but I learnt a lot about myself during that time. It moulded me into the kind of person and player that I am today.'

With Justin aged 35, retirement is something that was on his mind. He spoke of what he has planned in the future and how much of that involves the team in America he currently plays for.

'When I retire, I firstly want to end up with this team where I am now and hopefully playing another five years if I can. If not, if injury or something else happens, then I am working with the team in developing a youth academy. I want to help the club wherever I can, so right now I'm not sure where the path will take me. I'm open to all positions.

'We have got plans in place to achieve great things, so I hope we can do that as a team.'

As a closing remark, Justin summed up his time at Sunderland. He pointed out that although the season ended badly, he enjoyed many aspects of his time on Wearside and he was proud of what he achieved personally.

'Sunderland was great. I didn't enjoy everything about my time there, obviously not the way we were relegated, but it was great to be part of the club's history. I still look out for how the team are doing. It's disappointing where Sunderland are at the minute, but hopefully they can get back to the big time soon.'

Justin Hoyte was drafted in at the start of what would end up being a woeful season for Sunderland. He brought youthful energy to the side, and he got the consistent run of Premier League matches that would ultimately kick start a lengthy football career which is far from over yet.

He has a lot planned after he hangs up his boots, and he looks set to be a key part in the ongoing footballing revolution taking place in the USA.

TOMMY MILLER

Born in Shotton Colliery, County Durham, Tommy Miller began his youth career at Ipswich Town before moving, back nearer to his home, to Hartlepool United. A central-midfielder by trade, Tommy made his senior debut at Victoria Park, and he went on to make over 160 appearances and scored 41 goals for Hartlepool. This attracted interest from teams further up the league pyramid.

In fact, his next move would take him from the Third Division to the Premiership. Ipswich Town paid over £750,000 for Tommy in July 2001. He wouldn't feature much in this first season at Portman Road, with the club finishing 18th and consequently being relegated. However, he did get a taste of UEFA Cup football in November 2001. Tommy made his league debut in a 0-0 draw with Middlesbrough three weeks later.

The 2004-05 season was particularly fruitful for Tommy and Ipswich. He scored 15 goals and made 50 appearances as the Tractor Boys reached the Championship play-offs. They went on to lose 4-2 on aggregate to West Ham United, who eventually secured promotion by beating Preston North End 1-0 in the final.

Tommy rejected a contract extension at Ipswich amidst interest from clubs in higher divisions, including Sunderland. In July 2005 he put pen to paper on a two-year deal at the Stadium of Light. It would be a decent season for Tommy, but one to forget for Sunderland as they racked up just 15 points. It was a tough campaign for everyone on Wearside.

Despite starting the first few matches of the 2006-07 season, Tommy was down the pecking order of Roy Keane's side. He went out on loan to Preston North End for some of the season, and he made his final appearances for Sunderland in March 2007.

His next permanent move was back to a place he knew well. Tommy moved back to Ipswich Town. He had two more full seasons in Suffolk, playing over 35 times in both. His time at Ipswich ended and his next move was to Yorkshire. Staying in the Championship, Tommy moved to Sheffield Wednesday. From 2011-12, and for the next four seasons, Tommy turned out for a different club. He featured for Huddersfield Town, Swindon Town, Bury and finally Hartlepool United, where he made his 600th career appearance in 2015.

Looking back to his move to Wearside, Tommy explained how it came about and that the move suited him both professionally and personally.

He said. 'They'd just been promoted to the Premier League, I was at Ipswich at the time and we had just missed out on promotion. We came ever so close. It was a chance to move back up home, to be 10 to 15 minutes away from home. I'd been brought up as a Sunderland fan, I went to the games, and it was an opportunity I couldn't turn down. Everything added up and I signed for Sunderland, which was a dream come true as it was a team I had supported as a kid.'

Tommy had some experience from playing in the top flight at Ipswich Town earlier in his career, and when asked if he felt he was ready to play in the Premier League again, he said,

'I think so. I'd proved myself in the Championship over three years and in a couple of years I'd scored a few goals and I wanted to push myself in the league above. It was an ideal opportunity to do that with Sunderland.'

Mick McCarthy was the man to bring Tommy to the Stadium of Light, and he had fond memories of McCarthy's way of always being blunt and straight to the point.

'He's a straight talking guy. There's no hidden agenda with him. If he tells you you're rubbish he tells you straight. If you're playing well then he'll tell you. It was always black and white, I got on really well with him. I even lived next to him for a period of time whilst I was waiting for a house to be built. He was in one apartment and I was in the door opposite. It was a strange situation, but personally I got on with him very well.'

Tommy went into more detail of his living arrangements next to his new manager, and recalled what it was like to get a knock on the door from McCarthy when looking around his new home.

'It was strange at first, I didn't realise he lived around there. I went to view this apartment one day and I parked my car out in front in between two spaces, thinking no more of it. I was inside the flat being shown around and I was there saying "Yeah this is great for what I need at the moment."

'There was a bang on the door and the estate agent has answered it and it's Mick McCarthy. He then says, "Do you mind moving your f******* car," which was bizarre because I didn't know he lived there and I also didn't realise I was parked in someone else's space.

'The next day at training he was laughing and joking with me, but let me tell you now he was very serious at the time. We used to occasionally pass each other on the landing coming in and out, but he was a great bloke.'

Tommy joined Sunderland in the summer before the disappointing 2005-06 campaign. He spoke of what the mood of the squad was like in the build-up to the new season, and how the players were up for the challenge.

'The mood was good. It was on a high, they'd been promoted from the Championship to the Premier League. They were all buoyant and ready to test themselves. The lads at the club were in a great mood and they were ready to test themselves against the best. Everyone was looking forward to the challenge ahead.

'With the calibre of players coming in, I think the fans perhaps expected more. I think Mick was very limited with his budget, there weren't any high-budget signings as such which would set the world alight.'

It was clear that Tommy was hugely disappointed with the way the season went. It was a step up, which the Sunderland squad were unable to make.

'If you're going from the Premiership to the Championship, you need to invest. It's a huge jump. There is a big difference in quality. It was very disappointing the way the season panned out.'

Tommy admitted that the core Mick McCarthy had assembled was good, but it wasn't a core that was up to the standard required to keep Sunderland in the Premier League.

'You had Gary Breen who was still there, he was the captain, and Steven Caldwell too. Julio Arca, Liam Lawrence, Dean Whitehead too. They had a good core, but it was a Championship core of a team I would say.

'That's why they got promoted. What they were looking for the next year was to sign players who would improve on that. We didn't set the world alight, but not many people did that year. It was a struggle.'

Tommy was a regular feature in the Sunderland side during this season, playing 31 times in all competitions and scoring three goals. When talking about how the season was for him personally, he said:

'From a personal point of view, I don't think I played in a position that suited my strengths, which was getting forward and getting in the box. I realised early on that my position might need to change. I was playing alongside Dean Whitehead, who liked to get forward, he had energy, and I was having to do more of the defensive work, which was not completely my kind of play.'

Tommy added that he had more freedom elsewhere in his career, including during his time at Portman Road, as well as pointing out that if the 2004-05 season had played out differently, he may have stayed at Ipswich and had a more enjoyable season in the top flight.

'At Ipswich, I had a free role. We played a different kind of game. Don't get me wrong, I knew that at Sunderland I wasn't going to get the freedom and the opportunity to push forward, I just felt that I needed to adapt my game to Sunderland and to the Premier League in the situation where we were at the time.

'It's easy to say this, but I think if Ipswich had gone up instead of Sunderland it would have benefitted me a lot more. Obviously, I didn't know this at the time, and it's easy to say that now, but looking back and reflecting on how Sunderland played a different formation and we set up differently, our tactics were different.'

This was put down to having two very different managers at, first, Ipswich and then at Sunderland. Tommy felt that the style of play that was executed by Joe Royle at Ipswich was more beneficial to him than the football played by Mick McCarthy's Sunderland.

'Mick McCarthy is a totally different manager to Joe Royle, and look Royle could have taken Ipswich up and they would have needed to change their style of play for the Premier League. I don't think we would have changed it much, but I think we would have changed it slightly because you play against better teams and you don't get to have the ball as much as you do in the Championship.

'I feel that different managers and different characters come into play, I think I would have benefitted more had I gone up with Ipswich rather than joining Sunderland who had different tactics and different ideas which didn't suit me much."

During the 2005-06 season, Tommy found the back of the next on three occasions. One of these goals came in the first of Sunderland's three wins during the season. In September, Sunderland visited the Riverside Stadium for the Tees Wear Derby. The visitors ran out 2-0 winners, with Tommy opening the scoring with a close finish after just two minutes. Julio Arca curled in a free kick on the hour mark to seal the victory in what was a special day for Sunderland fans.

Tommy explained how it felt to score and to get a very important three points, and how everyone hoped it would be the kick start to the season that was desperately needed. The win on Teesside came a week after Sunderland were foiled in injury time by West Bromwich Albion at the Stadium of Light. Gary Breen's first-half header was cancelled out by Zoltan Gera to snatch a late point for the Baggies.

On the victory over Middlesbrough, Tommy said, 'The monkey was off our back. We finally got that first win and we thought that we would then push on and try to get some points on the board to make a mark in the league.

'It was a great feeling to beat Middlesbrough, obviously it's a bit of a local derby and there were lots of Middlesbrough fans around near where I lived. It was good to get it off our backs but we didn't really push on as much as we would have liked. The season wasn't great.'

As it was, Sunderland didn't kick on, and their next victory came in January 2006 in the form of a 1-0 win away to West Bromwich Albion. Tommy said that things could have been different if McCarthy was given the amount of financial support that other managers received before and after him.

'It's easier said than done. I always say that if Mick had been given the money that Sunderland would have stayed up. If he'd been given the money which previous managers had been given to spend then certainly Sunderland wouldn't have ended up where they are now in League One, which is an absolute disaster, as well as a financial disaster.

'It's one of them, but, like I said, with Mick he is a sound bloke. He knew what it would take to keep Sunderland in the Premier League.

'If you look at the amount of money which has been given to managers since Mick, it's ridiculous.'

Up until Derby County's 11-point season in 2007-08, Sunderland's 15-point total was a Premier League record. When asked what he thought went wrong during the season, Tommy answered frankly.

He said, 'I think we weren't good enough. At the end of the day, on the whole, as a squad, we weren't good enough. You are where you are and the table doesn't lie. If you go down you can't say, "Oh we were unlucky and we should have won that game here and there."

'In general, as a club, we just weren't good enough. It wasn't for a lack of effort or desire, I just think the quality wasn't there. We had the occasional player who would show a bit of flair and magic, but as a team we weren't good enough and that's why we were where we were in the table. We went down and it was a nightmare, it wasn't nice.'

The summer of 2006 saw big change on Wearside, but Tommy started the first three matches of the Championship season. He spoke of what it was like at Sunderland during the pre-season:

'I was looking forward to the Championship. I knew I could do it at that level from when I was at Ipswich. I wanted to get started and we were all keen to bounce back. There was a lot of talk around the club during the summer about possible changes and who would be the new manager. Niall Quinn did a bit in pre-season, there were all sorts of rumours flying around.'

Tommy added how he picked up an injury early in the season, which put him on the sidelines when Roy Keane was appointed manager.

'We started the season and I think it was about the third game against Plymouth Argyle. I got injured after about 60 minutes and we lost the match. It was ankle ligament damage, and I missed the next six weeks.

'Within that time, Roy Keane came in and he brought in three or four new players, most of these were midfielders. Dwight Yorke played in central midfield at the time, then there was Graham Kavanagh and Liam Miller.

'So, I knew it was going to be hard to get back into the team. Roy had money to spend and he was going to spend it. I can see from his side that he wanted to make changes, he'd seen the season before as a failure and he maybe wanted to bring in other characters to try and lift the spirits and get the club back up which, ultimately, he did.'

During his layoff, Tommy said he was kept informed about goings on at the club, but admitted that, as an injured player, he was of no use to Keane when he first stepped into the hot seat.

'I was always kept in the know, but I think the problem is that as an injured player, you're no good to a manager. If you're injured, you don't get disregarded, but you're no good to the manager at that time. The manager needs to focus on those who are fit; like I said, he had the money and was going to spend it. I was still in and around the set up and would go to the games, but I couldn't do anything about it because I was injured. It was a frustrating time and obviously I wanted to be part of it.

'Roy Keane was a massive player growing up, and I admired him. He was a fantastic player and I wanted to learn from him. It's a shame that once I was fit I didn't get the chance to show him what I could do.'

Tommy said that he could see his chances to play for Roy Keane would be limited, and that he knew he would probably be a player Keane wanted to move on.

'I thought I would get an opportunity, but Roy had his team set up. He knew who he wanted to play. With the amount of players he was bringing in, he perhaps needed to get rid of players to balance the books. Me being injured, coming back and struggling to get back into the team, he maybe saw me as someone to move on.

'He saw my future elsewhere, which was disappointing, but there was no falling out. I got on perfectly well with him, I trained hard to get back, I was doing everything I could to score goals in the reserve team, I just didn't really get the opportunity, hence why I went out on loan and then left the club at the end of my two-year contract.'

Away from Wearside, Tommy's career continued to thrive. In 2012 he joined Swindon Town, where he played for a footballing cult hero who would later be sat in the dug-out at the Stadium of Light. Paolo Di Canio signed Tommy Miller after leading the Robins to the League Two title. Tommy talked about what the often controversial Italian was like to work with.

He said, 'I love him. People ask me this a lot. He is a fantastic man and very passionate when goals are scored – and his antics on the sidelines – but he's also a very good coach. I thought I'd seen everything and learnt as much as I could in the game, but then I went to play for him and I was in my 30s learning new things.

'He was very demanding, passionate and intense, but I loved it. I loved going into training and learning from him. It was a bit like groundhog day sometimes, we would go over something repeatedly but it was working – he was getting results.

'We were top of the league in League One and I was probably as fit as I'd been since I was young. I really believed in everything he was doing, I trusted him. Yes, his man-management skills let him down, there's no doubt about that, you had to be mentally strong or you would go under the radar. As a man and a coach, I really enjoyed him and I got on well with him.'

Despite the success at Swindon, Tommy could sense that if Di Canio got a job at a club higher up the Football League pyramid, he would need to change his ways.

'I always knew at Swindon that if he ever got a bigger job, he would need to change. His man-management style let him down and he was very tough to certain individuals. I thought that if he went to a big club, like he did at Sunderland, you have players who are earning thousands and thousands of pounds; a lot more than lads at Swindon are earning, and they wouldn't take it. I knew that he would need to change if he went higher, and ultimately the lads obviously got together and forced him out at Sunderland. It was a shame, but that's how it is.'

Tommy was a big fan of many aspects of Di Canio's management style, but reiterated that at Sunderland he would have needed to change in order to fit in with a Premier League club.

'I said he would have to change, but I don't think he would. That's just how he was. In terms of everything else, he's Premiership. He does everything right. His attention to detail is superb, and, although his coaching was sometimes repetitive, it got results.

'His methods and ideas were sometimes crazy but you look back and see he was right. Although you question it at the time, you can look back now and see what he was trying to do. It was right. It's a shame to see him out of the game, but he needed to change, although it's sometimes hard to change what is within you. He's very set in his ways.'

Tommy started his career and made his professional debut for Hartlepool United, a team located just down the coast from Sunderland. His career came full circle in 2014 when, at the age of 35, he returned to Victoria Park. He would make 15 appearances to help his side avoid relegation out of the Football League.

Talking about this period in his career, Tommy had a lot of praise for Hartlepool for what the club had done for him at the start of his career.

'It was nice to get back to where it had started. I owe Hartlepool a lot. They gave me my chance to break through into football, and I will be forever grateful. It's a great club and a proper club. They were Division Four at the time and it was proper men's football. As a young kid coming through, it was great.'

His experience of playing men's football at a young age is one that he recommends young players in the current day to do. He felt that players who play in academies don't get the true experience of what it's like in the bread-and-butter of the Football League.

'I see a lot of young players coming through academies now, and academies, to me, are false to a certain level because there is no tackling. It's a case of "you have the ball and then we have the ball", kids need to go out and play football.

'Under-23s and under-18s need to go out and play men's football, and there is no better way to do that than in a lower-league club. Go to a League One, Two or National League club and play games at that level. It's a great way to toughen up and find out what playing real football is like.'

Tommy spoke of his return to Hartlepool, and the unfortunate circumstances that surrounded his first few matches back.

'Hartlepool was fantastic for me and it was great to go back before I retired. I still thought I had a lot to offer, but I think in my second or third game back I got injured against Cambridge. I tore my calf and I just couldn't get back.

'I kept on breaking down and re-tearing it. I got back towards the end of the season and played in one of the last games of the season, to make my 600th career appearance. I was just never the same after that injury.'

Tommy also had a few words to say about the manager who helped steer Hartlepool to safety:

'It was pleasing, Ronnie Moore came in and did a good job. He had a lot of games to save the club, and everyone would say he was a saviour and yes he did well, but he had a lot of games.

'That's not me knocking him, he did well to keep the club up, but it was a bit of "this is the Ronnie Moore show". For me being injured on the sidelines watching on, I was just desperate for the club to stay up.'

He added why he was particularly determined to get back into the side towards the end of the season, and how the numbers wouldn't add up for him if he didn't:

'I got back towards the end of the season to make it 600 games and I was pleased because I've got a bit of OCD so it would have bugged me to have been stuck on 599. I would never have lived it down if I finished on that. It would not add up, you would need to put me on in a wheelchair!'

Going back to his time at Sunderland, Tommy spoke of the few high points that intersected a disappointing season overall:

'It was disappointing, obviously, with the way it worked out. There were a few moments during the season, like the goal at Middlesbrough, and I scored in the home game with West Ham. The whole experience was disappointing.

'Getting relegated with your boyhood club wasn't great and, being a local, I would get things said to me from other people, saying, "What's going on at the club?" and "Why aren't you doing this and that?" but that's life. You need to be mentally strong and Sunderland is a massive football club.

'If you are doing well, there is no better place, but if you're struggling the fans will get on your back. It's like this everywhere, but at Sunderland it's very intense and passionate. You need to be thick-skinned.'

In summary, for his season on Wearside, Tommy said, 'Looking back, I wouldn't regret joining Sunderland. I pulled on the shirt and scored a few goals along the way, but how it ended was disappointing, it didn't go according to plan.'

Since retiring, Tommy has remained firmly involved in the game. He talked of what he did after hanging up his boots and what he has done since.

'I've got a coaching company up and running and I was going into schools. I was doing some alternative education, which is looking after children who weren't attending school, who were coming to me and we were educating them and then doing different activities in an afternoon.

'I am also the assistant manager of Spennymoor Town, and have been for the last four years. It's a fantastic club and it's going in the right direction. Behind the scenes, it is run better than some pro clubs I have been at. The chairman is very ambitious, he wants the club to go from strength to strength and to hopefully get to the Football League in the next few years.'

He spoke of the disappointment of the season being ended early due to the Coronavirus pandemic, and how Spennymoor Town were in a good position to bounce back from play-off heartache.

'I'm doing things like that, and I am enjoying it. It's a shame what happened with the season and it ending early. We were having a good season. We lost in the play-offs last year in the final against Chorley. They went up to the National League at our expense, but we'll get there one day.

'I had the flipside to the play-offs in my career. I got promoted to the Championship with Huddersfield. To be honest we, as in Spennymoor, probably weren't ready to go up. We would be going into the National League where every team is full time and we are only run on a part-time basis. Whether we would go full time straight away or not, we probably wouldn't have, and we might have given it a year to see how it goes.

'There is a lot to think about, in terms of costing and travel. There are a lot of teams in that league that are located in the south of England and that means taking overnight stops. We have this in our league though, we go to Kings Lynn who play in the National League North, believe it or not.'

Tommy is determined to move into management and get into the higher levels of football, a move which he is preparing for with his work at Spennymoor.

'It was disappointing, but we'll go again and one day it might happen for us. I've also just completed one of my coaching licences, which is one to get ticked off. We'll see what is around the corner; ultimately, I want to get into management and do so at the highest level I can, so we will see what happens.'

Tommy Miller fulfilled the dream of every football fan – to play for his childhood club. It may have been in a disappointing season, but it's clear he thoroughly enjoyed every match he played in. His love for the game has transferred from his playing into his coaching, and in Spennymoor Town he is part of a club that is ambitious enough to have their sights set firmly on the Football League. Tommy is as down to earth as they come, and he has plenty still to offer the world of football.

PART 4

2006-10: BACK TO THE PROMISED LAND, AGAIN

The 2006-07 season was spent back in the Championship and, after a significant clear out of players, Sunderland were down to the bare bones. Niall Quinn became chairman and fronted a consortium that took over the club. Quinn was also the manager for the first few matches, getting things in place for Roy Keane to take over permanently.

When Keane was appointed, Sunderland were rock bottom of the Championship with no points and were out of the League Cup, although they had registered their first win of the season with a 2-0 victory over West Bromwich Albion at the Stadium of Light. What followed in the next eight months was a turnaround the likes of which is seen rarely in professional football.

Sunderland lay 12th at the turn of the year, following a 1-0 home defeat to Preston North End on 30 December. It would be their last defeat until April. A remarkable surge up the table in the second half of the season saw Sunderland lose just one of their last 19 matches, beating promotion rivals Derby County, Wolverhampton Wanderers and West Brom on the way. Promotion was all but sealed with a dramatic 3-2 win over Burnley at the end of April, meaning that by the time they travelled to Luton Town for the last match of the season Sunderland knew that a win would seal the title.

And win they did. The hosts, who were already relegated, were beaten 5-0. Cue the celebrations after another immediate return to the top flight.

The 2007-08 season came around and Sunderland's return to the Premier League began. The opening few months went from winning one and then losing three or four as Sunderland gradually acclimatised to the league. Their 15th-place finish was largely down to a stubborn home record, especially after Christmas. Sunderland won six out of ten matches at the Stadium of Light, including four in a row. From the end of January onwards, Sunderland stayed out of the bottom three, securing their safety with two matches to spare.

What made life tough for Sunderland this season was the away form. Keane's side won just two of their matches on the road, the first of which came at the end of March. Their wretched form included a 7-1 demolition at the hands of Everton in

November, a disappointing 2-0 defeat at Newcastle as well as being held to a 0-0 draw at rock-bottom Derby County – the side who would go on to beat the lowest points total set by Sunderland in 2006. The Rams finished the season on just 11 points.

In terms of a first season back in the Premier League, it couldn't have gone much better for Roy Keane and Sunderland. He continued the trend of bringing together a hard-working team that wouldn't set the world alight but would get the job done.

The following campaign brought with it plenty of ups and downs, both on and off the pitch. Sunderland made a slow start, and by November Roy Keane was no longer at the club and Ricky Sbragia took over until the end of the season.

Before this, Sunderland had beaten Newcastle at home for the first time in decades, thanks to a fierce free kick from Kieran Richardson and a cool finish from on loan Djibril Cisse.

Under Spragia, Sunderland picked up form over Christmas and New Year. Two defeats in ten had Sunderland in the top half of the table in February, before a slump set in. The Black Cats lost nine of their last 12 league matches, meaning that on the last day of the season they were looking elsewhere for the fortunes of Hull City and Newcastle. Fortunately, all three sides lost and Sunderland finished the season in 16th, three points worse off than the previous campaign.

Over the summer, Sunderland would need a new permanent manager. They found their man in Steve Bruce, who spent almost £30 million on new players. These signings included Darren Bent and Lee Cattermole, and the latter would go on to be a staple of the football club for years to come.

The season started well, with Sunderland lying eighth in November after six wins from 13 matches. Once again, the home form dominated, but after a 1-0 win against Arsenal on 21 November, Sunderland wouldn't win again until 9 March, dropping from eighth to 14th. This sparked a mini revival, and Sunderland rose to tenth in the table after a 1-0 win away to Hull City, before fading into a final finish of 13th.

Darren Bent finished the season on 25 league goals, making him the first Sunderland player to pass 20 goals in a season since Kevin Phillips in 2000. Steve Bruce had put together a solid team, and for the first time in a decade a genuine clinical goalscorer was plying his trade at the Stadium of Light.

TOBIAS HYSEN

Tobias Hysen was born in March 1982 in Gothenburg, Sweden. A left-winger by trade, his youth career involved time at Ubbhults and Lundby, with him making his professional debut for the latter.

In 1999 he joined BK Hacken, a team based in Gothenburg. Tobias played over 60 matches and scored 13 goals for his home-town club. This included in the Allsvenskan, the top flight of Swedish football, as well as the second tier after Hacken's relegation in 2001, otherwise known as the Superettan.

For the start of the 2004 season, Tobias moved to play his football in Stockholm, for Djurgården IF. In the next three years, he would score 34 goals in over 100 league, cup and European tournament games. It was form like this that attracted the attention of newly relegated Sunderland in the summer of 2006.

Tobias signed on the dotted line at the Stadium of Light during Niall Quinn's brief tenure as manager. Battling for the left-wing position, with Roy Keane signing Ross Wallace, Tobias featured 27 times in all competitions as he helped Sunderland to the Championship title. He also scored four times, with his first coming on just his second appearance for the club in a 1-1 draw against Leicester City at the Stadium of Light.

Departing Sunderland and England in August 2007, Tobias returned to his native Sweden. His six years at IFK Göteborg took him back to the town of his birth, where he scored 85 goals in over 200 appearances across seven seasons. During this period, he won the Allsvenskan in 2007 and the Swedish cup in 2008 and 2013 with the team from Gothenburg.

In 2014 Tobias took the opportunity to play in the Chinese Super League with Shanghai SIPG. During two seasons in China, he scored 31 times in 55 appearances. Turning down the option for a third season with Shanghai, Tobias returned to IFK Göteborg for another three seasons. He picked up where he'd left off at his home-town club, scoring 24 goals in nearly 100 appearances.

On top of a good club record, Tobias featured 34 times for his country and found the net on ten occasions. This included two goals in a 5-3 defeat to Germany in Stockholm during a FIFA World Cup 2014 qualifying match.

Tobias spoke firstly of how his move to Wearside came about, as well as how disappointment at missing out on the 2006 World Cup led him to want a change of scenery and a new challenge.

'The two years prior to going to Sunderland were two of the best I had in my career. In 2004/05 I was playing in Stockholm for Djurgården IF, winning the cup twice and the league once.

'Then I was thinking of leaving in the winter between 2005 and 2006, but there was a World Cup coming up and I thought staying in Sweden and playing in the Swedish League would give me a better chance of being picked for the squad.

'That didn't happen, I was a reserve at home. In the summer I just felt I needed a change. My form was starting to dip a little bit and I was thinking that I needed a change of scenery.

Sunderland came in for Tobias four games into a season in which they had made a disastrous start. The Black Cats lost away at Coventry City and Southend United and at home to Birmingham City and Plymouth Argyle, leaving the club rock bottom of the Championship under chairman and manager Niall Quinn.

This start didn't deter Tobias, and he wanted to join Sunderland to help get the club back to the Premier League.

'That's when Sunderland came in and made an inquiry and a bid. Then I thought, they just lost four games in the Championship, they were relegated from the Premier League with the lowest amount of points ever at that point the year before, but I thought it's a big club with a massive stadium and massive fan base. If the club can get back on their feet it will be the perfect place to be at.'

The chance to play football in England like his father before him – Glenn Hysen played for Liverpool from 1989 to 1992 – was something Tobias didn't want to pass up.

'I thought that it's the change of scenery I wanted. It's England, I've always loved English football growing up, watching it on TV, and with my dad playing in England for a few years. When they came in and made it clear that the transfer was going to be able to go through, I just went with my gut. I thought "I needed a change, so let's go for it."'

Tobias gave an assessment of what he thought about Sunderland prior to joining, and how he received a confidence boost from Niall Quinn upon signing at the Stadium of Light.

'When you know football, you know it. When you get relegated with a team, obviously the start of the season is going to be important in the year after. If you start off like Sunderland did, there will be troubles and challenges on the way.

'I also thought that the club is so big, and it is a massive task to turn things around, but when Niall Quinn was the manager and chairman he told me that we were going to get in a manager and he is going to be a big name, we're going to make some new signings. We were not going to be near the bottom at the end of the year. He said that I was one of the first pieces of the puzzle to get new players in and get things turned around.'

He added that, despite his optimism, the choice to join Sunderland was a difficult one; and one which wasn't helped by a League Cup defeat, which happened on the day he arrived in England.

'I thought, "well, I don't think Sunderland will be at the bottom of the table, but obviously it wasn't an easy decision. They were bottom of the league and had been losing games. As I was touching down at the airport, they got knocked out of the cup by Bury, so I was thinking, "hmm, OK, but anyway I'm here, let's go and try to help bring some energy to the team and come in with a positive attitude, and try to get the team going again."'

Shortly after Tobias signed for Sunderland, Roy Keane was unveiled as Sunderland's new manager. He spoke of what it was like in the first few weeks of the new regime.

'When a person like that, with the reputation that he has, you're always thinking how is this going to end up, and what is he going to be like. It's a different thing to be a player and a manager.

'He set his standards straight away, he signed a couple of players and he made sure that everyone who was in the squad knew that there was going to be different demands.'

Tobias noted that the respect which he commanded as a player had been brought into Keane's management style, and he saw an instant improvement in the squad's morale and ability.

'He wasn't going to have us going to Bury and losing because that was out of the question. Obviously, with the new players coming in the squad improved, the training sessions were getting better and you could see straight away the respect that he had for the reputation he had as a player.'

He talked of a version of a honeymoon period at Sunderland, as the Black Cats won five of Roy Keane's first nine games in charge.

'That helped everyone to raise their games just a bit. With all that happening, it created a snowball effect. Everyone started rolling and things got better. To be honest, in the first couple of games, things were going on their own with the energy he brought but it didn't really settle until January, I would say.'

Sunderland had improved greatly in the lead up to Christmas, and after a 2-0 win over Leeds United at the Stadium of Light they sat 11th in the table. However, Tobias said that it was the first games of the New Year and certain signings in the January transfer window that set up a remarkable end of the season.

'We were doing OK in the first 20 or so games, but after the New Year period, with games against Preston and Leicester, was when it really kicked off. He brought in Jonny Evans, Carlos Edwards, Danny Simpson, and when those three came in things settled more. It's like three missing pieces were there. We could start winning games on a regular basis.'

The run was up there with some of the best in the Championship's history. Between New Year's Day and the end of the season, Sunderland lost one of their last 20 league matches. This one defeat was away at Colchester United, but the 3-1 defeat in April 2007 didn't derail the promotion push.

Tobias talked of this defeat and how it was important for Sunderland not to lose focus for the two remaining matches. They did not, beating Burnley 3-2 at the Stadium of Light before wrapping up the title with a 5-0 win at already-relegated Luton Town.

'It was always going to be like that. It doesn't matter where you play or how you play, it's always going to be difficult. There is always going to be that odd game when you don't turn up. Its sometimes about thinking, "OK we've won 15 out of our last 16, we're going to keep going," and then you forget the basics and forget what got you on that run.

'You'll take that on the chin and remember for the next game and think, "we can't just go out there and think it will settle itself". I think we won about 18 out of the last 22; obviously, if you win that many games and get three points every week, its going to end up looking pretty good.'

Tobias scored his first goal for Sunderland in a 1-1 draw against Leicester City in September 2006. When asked about this, he said it was good to get a game under his belt.

'For me personally, I was happy to get to play my first game under Roy Keane. When he came in, he signed Ross Wallace and he wanted to give him a chance and he was playing a lot. I came on against Leicester City and it was my first real chance and first couple of minutes under him as the new manager. For me, it was more like giving him a tough choice of who was he going to play.

'When you play left wing, your main role isn't scoring goals, it's setting other people up. obviously if you can help the team by scoring some goals too, it's always a good thing. I was happy to be able to contribute to the team.

'We were 1-0 down and I got us a point in the end. For me, it was more about showing the manager that he had played Ross for three or four games, now he could play me. In the end, I managed to get a few games in under my belt and make sure that when Ross couldn't play, or was off his game, I could come into the side and do the same.'

Tobias went on to talk about what his life was like living in Sunderland and how he found it difficult to settle in:

'The life itself wasn't that big. England and Sweden have very similar culture and lifestyle. The main thing was that for the first time I was without my friends and family, it was a bit further away than normal.

'It was more about the social life and getting new friends. In Sweden I moved from Gothenburg to Stockholm and things kind of sorted themselves out. I was playing well, and I made a lot of new friends in Stockholm, but I was thinking things would pan out.

'Looking back, maybe I should have done a bit more trying to settle in. In the end, leaving at the end of the first season, it was more down to wanting to get back to the normal circumstances with friends and family rather than the playing. If it was just the playing, I could have played somewhere else.

'Maybe I wouldn't have gotten the time at Sunderland, but I could have gone somewhere else and back to the Championship to settle into the English football system.'

He added that his return to Sweden after one year at Sunderland had nothing to do with how and where he lived in the north east of England.

'For me, it was more just I wanted to go back and start over. The life in the North East had nothing to do with it, I thought it was beautiful. We were living in Durham and we'd go to Sunderland and, I know I shouldn't say, Newcastle as well. It was a big city with everything it had to offer.

'Sunderland was beautiful, down by the sea. It wasn't about that, it was more about the life. It wasn't really what we expected, but that was more of our own fault.'

Getting back to matters on the pitch, Tobias talked of the change in mood around the club as the success of the team built throughout the season:

'It was good, as it always is. When you're the member of a squad which is consistently winning you come in and people are happy, the backroom staff are happy, the medical staff are happy. Everyone is happy. When I first came in, everything was down. There was a feeling that something needed to happen.

'But then, when things started moving in the right direction, everyone was feeling happier. When you spoke to the journalists, they were happy, so was everyone in the media department at the club. It goes without saying, when you're going well, everyone is happy.'

Tobias felt that the events on the pitch didn't always reflect the mood in the dressing room and added that this is something that changes little during the season.

'In a dressing room, there will always be ups and downs. I think what is special about the dressing room is that it is always going to be the same. Even when things weren't going to plan, you're never not friends or smiling and laughing. It's easier to do this when you're winning, but that's the thing which goes in a dressing room.

'Everyone who has played in a team sport knows that results don't always affect the spirit. It's easier to be happy when things are going well, the important thing is keeping it going when things aren't.'

He said that the joy of seeing Sunderland winning matches after such a poor period in the club's history was enough to make a lot of people happy and improve the mood on Wearside.

'I would say everything around the club was changing, and people were getting their hopes up. The biggest change around the club was the buzz of winning games after a year and a half of losing lots of matches.'

During the 2006-07 campaign, Sunderland had two good left-wing players in the squad. Tobias was one, with the other being Ross Wallace, who was signed by Roy Keane. When asked if the competition between two players was positive or negative, Tobias said it is best to take things into consideration.

He said, 'You can look at it two ways, for the competition and for the squad it's always better than for the two players. If one has a bad day then you can put the other in and he will do a job. If one gets injured, you'll have one in reserve that you can put in and he can play a few games. Personally, you want to play every game.

'If I would have said for my own benefit that I would have been on my own, maybe with one other play, but it would be a clear choice of, "You're number one and you're number two,' and the number two would have been happy about it.

'With me and Ross, it was more like he was the number one or he was one and a half and I was two and a half. He wasn't that much better that I would look at him and say, "I'm never going to play if he's fit," but at the same time he was the first choice and he was playing games. For me personally, it wasn't the best situation, but for the squad it was perfect.

'That's what you need to look at. Even though you look to yourself first but looking at it from the outside it was perfect.'

When joining Sunderland, Tobias said that he could notice the impact that the previous relegation season had left on those players who remained at the club.

'Things needed to change; some players left after the relegation. It's easy to say when you know what the result was, but many of the players there were a little bit affected by the way things had gone so badly for such a long time.'

Despite some of the players who left during this season, perhaps being good enough to get the club back into the Premier League, Tobias saw that the club needed change on the pitch.

'Some of the players who left during that season were great players. You could see in training and in different games that these players would easily be able to play in the Premier League.

'However, at the time and at that club, they had pretty much hit a brick wall. The baggage which came with being relegated and losing a couple of games at the start of the season was something which they couldn't get back from.

'That's why I thought it was very important to get in that change of player and getting people in and going out. I think it would have been hard to turn things around with the exact same players.

'Having said that, I think the players who left could have turned it around because they were good enough, but just not at that time.'

Tobias summed up his time at Sunderland, saying that despite not playing his best football at the Stadium of Light, it was an enjoyable and successful season.

'Playing wise, I played much better at other places. We won the league, I was involved in 28 games and when you look at the squad as a whole, not many players featured more than that.'

He added that he learned a lot about himself as a player during his 12 months on Wearside, and how it is only when he looks back now that he truly appreciates it.

'Obviously, this was partially to do with players coming and going through the season, but we won the league and it was a very good year for me. At the time I might not have appreciated it that much, but I learned a lot about myself and about preparing more mentally than in terms of physicality and ability.

'I think I did well in the games I did play, but mentally I could have prepared myself a little bit better. I could have had a bit more patience and thought that, "this is what I need to do, and this is what has to change".'

Tobias said that the benefit of hindsight is a key aspect of how to assess his time at Sunderland, adding that it is no secret he played his best football elsewhere.

'I was 25 at the time and it's easy to say now, as someone who is a bit over 30 and closing into 40, that you could have done this and that, because if you could do that then everyone would do it. I had my best playing days at other clubs, and I think everybody understands that.'

After returning to Sweden, Tobias enjoyed seven years at IFK Göteborg; winning the league and the cup with his home-town club. In 2013 he took up the opportunity to play for Shanghai SIPG in the Chinese Super League.

Talking about this experience, Tobias mentioned the change in culture and how the two seasons he played in China were different from one another.

'China was completely different, and the interesting part was that the first and second year were completely different to each other. The first year was completely Chinese, everyone in the staff and the owners were Chinese apart from the goalkeeper coach, who was Ian Walker who played for Tottenham.

'We had four foreign players, as every club had, but the training methods and everything was influenced by what they had done before, so it was a little bit old fashioned. We were playing well, many of the players were very good and better than I expected.

'We were living outside of the city, a long way outside of Shanghai, so it was hard to settle in that area.'

Tobias pointed out how much of the club changed from the first year through to the second, both on and off the pitch. This included the background staff becoming more international.

'However, after the first year, the club wanted to take the next step. It was bought by a company called SIGP and the club was renamed Shanghai SIGP. Then they brought in Sven Goran Eriksson and he brought with him a completely different staff. There was a Swedish doctor, assistant manager, the medical staff were Italians, South Africans.'

He talked of how his time in China was a learning curve and how it allowed him to develop as a player and a person:

'The training methods went back to what I see as normal. For the Chinese players, it was different. The two years in China were very educational for me as a player and as a human being. Learning and adapting to different cultures, you get a bigger understanding of different things, especially when it comes to culture.'

Tobias returned to Sweden and played another three years with IFK Göteborg before hanging up his boots for good. He talked of his thought process in his retirement and what he has done since.

'I retired after the 2018 season; since then there have been a few things. When I got back from China, I was going to be 34 that year. I had a two-year deal with the option of a one-year extension, to get three years in total.

'I thought to myself, I'm going to be 36 at the end of that. My plans were to retire at the end of those three years, which I did. I had some problems with my knees, and I couldn't train as much, so my ability was degrading. It wasn't fun anymore.

'I decided pretty early, so I looked into different things. In the last year of playing I was looking into what I would do. I have a sports restaurant here in Gothenburg where we show sports. It's become a great place for the Gothenburg fans to watch all the home and away games. We have an ice hockey team here and we show their games, and the Premier League from England."

Tobias also spoke of a new football team that he has helped to set up, to make sure he's never too far away from the sport that has been a big part of his life.

'Apart from that, we have founded a new club here and it's about 25 minutes out from Gothenburg. We started in the Eighth Division in Sweden, and we got promoted from that division by winning it and into the seventh. Hopefully, we will be going for promotion again when things are back to normal.

'That's the footballing side sorted, and then some other small things I have been working on: football manager Sweden is a website which me and some friends have taken over. We are trying to revive the site with some new things. It's a bit of work, some voluntary stuff and of course the football just to try and keep in with the game a bit.'

As a closing line for his time at Sunderland, Tobias said that it was a challenge but one that he enjoyed – both on and off the pitch.

'It was good but challenging, both playing wise and as a person. It was good in a way that we won a lot of games, were able to get promoted and I was able to play with some great players and had a great manager. It was challenging in the way that I was always first choice in my career, but at Sunderland I needed to adapt and understand what it was like to not play week in and week out.

'Also, as a person, getting to handle the fact that friends and family weren't always going to be there. This was harder than I maybe thought when I left. It was good and challenging, both on and off the pitch.'

Tobias Hysen was one of the more exciting players to watch at the Stadium of Light. He went to Wearside with a good CV and he left with a Championship winner's medal added to it. He made a name for himself in three different countries and will always be seen as a key piece in the puzzle during a successful season at Sunderland.

DANNY HIGGINBOTHAM

Beginning his career with Manchester United, Danny Higginbotham notched almost 400 appearances in a 17-year career. A key member of Sunderland's Premier League survival in the 2007-08 season, Higginbotham moved to the Stadium of Light in August 2007 for £2.5 million. Making 21 appearances as Sunderland secured 15th position in their first season back in the top flight after promotion from the Championship under Roy Keane, Higginbotham was signed to bolster a defence which was looking under-prepared for life in the Premier League. He could play full-back or centre-back, enjoying some regular spells in the side.

Higginbotham was signed by Roy Keane after the 2007/08 season with Sunderland 14th in the table after two defeats from their opening four league games. He spoke highly of the club and how his decision to move to Wearside was an easy one.

'I had just had a good year at Stoke and was captain and enjoying my football, but I was eager to get back to the Premier League. When I heard of the interest of Sunderland it was an easy decision. I had played there many times and it was always a great atmosphere and great club. Added on to that the chance to work with Roy Keane as my manager was too good to turn down. I was an apprentice at Manchester United when Keane was one of the best central-midfield players in the world and it was an honour to join Sunderland and to work under him.

Higginbotham has cherished memories of the period he spent at Sunderland, yet he feels it could have turned out better.

'I should have done a lot better than what I did and the only person to blame for that was myself. Obviously, the goal against Newcastle was special, as all derby goals are, as well as the goals against Middlesbrough and Aston villa. The team spirit was magnificent, and the way Roy Keane drove you on was shown by the amount of late goals we scored, and we ended up staying up quite comfortably in the end.

Most footballers tend to ply their trade in more than one position, being adaptable to various situations which their manager may require them to play in. Danny was no exception to this.

His ability with his chosen foot gave him more opportunity to make more appearances throughout his career. He was used in two positions across the Sunderland back line, featuring as a centre-back and left-back. Whilst in these positions, Danny played alongside Danny Collins, Nyron Nosworthy and Jonny Evans, three other players who will be fondly remembered for their time at Sunderland.

Danny said how he was able to keep on playing in the middle of the defence when the left-back position was occupied, and vice versa.

'This happened at most clubs. I preferred centre-back without question but because I was left footed and could play in both positions you never really got to settle in one position, but on the other hand because I could play the two positions it meant that you were involved in more games.'

Danny is part of the elite club of players who have scored in a Sunderland shirt against the old enemy from up the coast. He enjoyed it as much as any other player who has had the pleasure to do this, but what makes it special for him is that he very nearly didn't play. His goalscoring boots were polished off in a training session just hours before the big kick-off.

He spoke about the build-up to the match, and how his manager put faith in him after the session during the week.

'It was incredible. We had worked on shape on the Thursday and I wasn't in the starting XI. Then on the Friday we always had a very competitive small game and I managed to score two or three. On the Saturday I was named in the starting line-up and managed to score. Afterwards Roy Keane was asked about my goal and he said he fancied me to score due to Friday's game. That was the thing with Roy. He was always watching and looking ahead, and this is a great example. It was just a shame we couldn't hold onto the lead.'

Danny looks back fondly on his time at the club, with praise in particular for his old manager.

'I had no issues at all at the club. I also believe that Roy Keane doesn't get the credit he deserves for his time at Sunderland. He took the team from bottom of the championship to the Premier League and kept the club there.'

Danny spoke of the attitude which the Irishman installed into the squad, and how it became a squad in which he was proud to be a part of.

'We trained how we played and that's something that unfortunately you don't see at every club. He got the best out of the team that season and as a player he was competitive, and having him as my manager made me understand even more in terms of desire and commitment what made him such a world-class player and it helped me a lot in the rest of my career.'

His time at Sunderland was relatively short, but Danny admitted that when his departure came it was at a good time in his career, with personal frustrations growing.

'I should have done better than what I did and, as I've said before, the only person to blame was myself. Sunderland were happy to let me move on and I think it suited everyone. I'm not one for staying at a club just to pick my money up but not play.'

He explained how a talk with Keane helped along a move away – back to one of his old clubs – and that it was vital in getting his career back on track.

'I chatted with Roy and I got the sense he was happy for me to move. Going back to Stoke kick-started my career again, but I was happy that I have had time at Sunderland, although I believe I didn't do myself justice.'

Danny was a player who always put a shift in when playing in the red and white of Sunderland. He was aware of what Sunderland fans wanted to see in their players.

The fans at Sunderland, like those of any football club, want to see their players work hard for their shirt. This, added with the odd important goal, would be enough to make any player a cult hero; and not just at Sunderland.

About the fans and what they want to see in a footballer, Danny said, 'Scoring against two local rivals always helps, but I found the fans incredibly passionate. They demand hard work and commitment and as long as you give, that there wouldn't be an issue.'

He was complimentary of the fans in this season and, despite losing more games at the Stadium of Light than most would have wanted, they witnessed their club register several vital victories on home turf.

One of these matches was a dramatic 3-2 win over Middlesbrough which all but sealed Sunderland's survival. Danny scored the equaliser in the sixth minute, teaming up with fellow defender and name sake Danny Collins to loop a header over Brad Jones in the Boro goal. This came after Tuncay Sanli fired the visitors into the lead with just four minutes on the clock.

Michael Chopra gave Sunderland the lead shortly before the break, only for Alfonso Alvez to restore parity in the second half. The match came a week after a disappointing 2-0 defeat at the hands of Newcastle, meaning the importance of three points couldn't be understated.

In the first of five minutes of injury time, late-goal merchant Daryl Murphy headed home the winner, the last in a long line of late goals scored throughout that season by the Irishman and Sunderland in general.

'We were newly promoted, and the atmosphere was great and the togetherness with the fans was brilliant and it helped us so much home and away.'

Club legend Niall Quinn was installed as chairman by the time Danny joined the club, yet it was after leaving Sunderland that he started seeing more of the former SAFC striker.

'I only saw Niall a few times but have since seen him quite a bit when he was working at Sky. He is an absolute gentleman.'

Danny is a Manchester United supporter and has been since he was young. His time at Sunderland coincided with two legends of the game who were a vital part of the Red Devil's treble-winning season of 1998-99.

Dwight Yorke and Andy Cole were brought in by Roy Keane, and during the 2007-08 season the pair were stand-out players within the dressing room. They had hundreds and hundreds of appearances between them by the time they were reunited at Sunderland, something that is always useful to turn to in the dressing room.

'These were two of my heroes growing up as a Manchester United fan and I was an apprentice there when Andy and Dwight were an unstoppable partnership. They were great in the dressing room. Very humble despite what they had done in the game and they gave everything for the cause and were a great influence.'

Sometimes in a dressing room you get players who stand out more than others. This can have its pros and cons, but Danny felt that this wasn't something he needed to deal with at Sunderland. Ultimately, it is what helped make the squad of this era into the well-oiled machine that Roy Keane had in mind.

'It was more of a team effort and it was great that when you went out onto the pitch it was a collective rather than an individual group.'

It was a short summary, but the few words Danny gave were fitting to a man who enjoyed his football and rarely left anything out on the pitch.

His time at Sunderland was one of the shorter spells for a player to have at the club, yet Danny considered it to be a learning curve. It was one which, in comparison to other seasons in the Premier League, was far more successful than others. Danny was a key part of this, as most Sunderland fans will agree.

When asked about how he felt his one season at Sunderland went, Danny was frank but fair. He said, 'I met some great people and learnt a lot about myself all in one season.'

Danny went back to Stoke City during the 2008-09 campaign as the Potters rose and established themselves as a Premier League side alongside Sunderland. Like at Sunderland, he became part of a tough unit of a team. In his first season, Stoke were somewhat of a surprise package, turning the Britannia Stadium into a fortress. Their team of strong, physical players would become a trademark over the course of the Potters' time in the Premier League, long after Danny departed in 2013.

Various loan spells at other clubs including Ipswich Town and Nottingham Forest were followed by a permanent switch to Sheffield United in 2013. The last two moves of his playing career took Danny closer to home, with Chester and finally Altrincham rounding off his CV.

Since hanging up his boots Danny has moved over to the media side of the game. His work on Sky Sports allowed him to use his wealth of playing experience to critique the sport, which he has given so much time to.

It was not the longest stay on Wearside for the man who represented Gibraltar on the international stage, yet he was part of a Sunderland squad that worked hard for each other and was, in hindsight, one of the most successful groups of players in the club's recent history.

His solid defensive displays and important goals have made Danny Higginbotham a name that will always be fondly remembered on Wearside. Any goalscorer against Newcastle will be remembered well at Sunderland, and Danny will be no exception.

KENWYNE JONES

Born in the Caribbean, more specifically Point Fortin in Trinidad & Tobago, in 1984, Kenwyne Jones would go on to ply his trade across three continents. He would leave a positive mark in all three of them.

A tall tower of a centre-forward, Kenwyne started his footballing career at nearby Joe Public in 2002 at the age of 18. His next club was W Connection FC, where he scored a remarkable 30 goals in 31 appearances. It was this knack for finding the goal that attracted attention from England, and Kenwyne soon swapped the beaches of the Caribbean for the south coast of England.

Southampton snapped up Kenwyne in 2004 and he spent three years in Hampshire, during which time he scored 19 goals in 71 appearances. This stint at Southampton also saw Kenwyne loaned out to Sheffield Wednesday and Stoke City, scoring goals at both. His chance to prove himself at the top tier of English football came in 2007, thanks to newly promoted Sunderland's search for a striker.

Roy Keane was piecing together a side which would have enough about it to survive in the Premier League. It was a side full of goals at Championship level, but, as anyone associated with football will tell you, the Premier League is a stern step up.

It could be said that the signing of Kenwyne Jones was a risk – a 23-year-old forward who was then untested in one of football's hardest divisions. Fortunately for Sunderland, and for the man himself, he didn't take long to settle in.

Less than half an hour into his debut, the man from Trinidad had found the back of the net and unveiled his signature somersault celebration to Wearside. The fans instantly took to him; it looked as though Sunderland had finally bagged a striker who was physical, an aerial presence and good with his feet.

Kenwyne said that the chance to play in England was something that he couldn't pass up. He spoke of how his entry into English football saw him move around a lot after landing in Southampton.

'As a foreigner, I wanted to have a great football career and experience, so after spending three years at Southampton, the opportunity arose to go to Sunderland, so I grabbed at it.'

The move from the Caribbean to the south coast is not a well-trodden path to say the least, and at the age of 19 Kenwyne would have been one of the youngest to do so. When asked how he found the transition to English football, he said, 'I thought it was fantastic, I wanted to play football, so it didn't matter where I went.'

It was this attitude to the game that made Kenwyne a fan favourite at the majority of clubs he turned out for.

Kenwyne would go on to score over 130 goals during his playing career and will be remembered as a towering 6ft 2in centre-forward with a superb celebration. However, as Kenwyne said, it wasn't always this way. It was arguably his build or maybe a keen eye for finding the back of the net that cemented Kenwyne's place as a striker.

'I was naturally a midfielder, but over the course of my youth I learned to play different positions and in the end being a striker stuck.'

Kenwyne joined a Sunderland team that had worked hard on and off the pitch since a barnstorming rise to the Championship title. They did so without a talismanic striker who bagged 20+ goals. David Connolly came out on top in the scoring charts with 13, closely followed by Daryl Murphy on ten.

He was the sought-after striker the team needed, and he explained that during the campaign the atmosphere with his fellow team-mates was mainly positive.

'I thought the mood in the dressing room was fantastic, the players had a really good bond.'

Kenwyne was of course signed by Roy Keane, for whom the 2007-08 season would be his first and only full campaign as manager at Sunderland. Keane installed a strong work ethic into the side and during the season would piece together a side which wasn't the most technically gifted but worked hard for each other.

'Roy's style was very demanding on the field of play, but off the field it was really relaxed like it should be.

After scoring seven goals in his first Premier League season and helping Sunderland to a respectable 15th-place finish, Kenwyne was once again the leading man during the 2008-09 season.

During this campaign, journeyman and often controversial forward El Hadji Diouf joined Sunderland on loan. He was a player whom Kenwyne picked out as the biggest character in the dressing room.

'Everyone was a character, but I think Diouf was top of the pile, he was too funny.'

From a fans perspective, it always seemed as though Kenwyne was a popular character within the dressing room and a player who the rest of squad could enjoy playing alongside.

He solidified this opinion, saying, :I've never had a problem with any of my team-mates, I thought of everyone as family.'

Another loan signing, who will probably be more fondly remembered by the majority of Sunderland than Diouf, was Djibril Cisse.

The Frenchman scored 11 times in 38 matches in all competitions for Sunderland, including two goals against fierce rivals Newcastle. His goals, along with ten from Kenwyne, kept Sunderland afloat despite a poorer campaign.

The Black Cats finished 16th and sacked manager Roy Keane before Christmas. Kenwyne said that it was a shame Djibril didn't stay at the club longer; however, the season he was there he was well thought of.

'I think it could've been greater if he was there another year, but for the time he was there I enjoyed it.'

Roy Keane departed the club in November 2008 following a 4-1 home defeat to Bolton Wanderers. This was the fifth defeat in six games, a run which saw Sunderland slip from ninth to 18th. Kenwyne admitted that the run of poor form meant that the Irishman's sacking was inevitable.

'I guess based on how things were going with the results that was the only outcome, but I enjoyed his style, I think he's misunderstood.'

After Roy Keane was sacked, coach Ricky Sbragia took over for the rest of the season. A relatively fruitful December made sure that Sunderland would just about have enough points to avoid the drop. This was despite a poor second half of the season in which Sunderland won just three out of 17 games after new year.

Kenwyne scored in two of these three wins, including the winner against Fulham in January and the first in a 2-0 win over Stoke City in February, both at the Stadium of Light. It was a disappointing second half of the campaign, but it was one that ended in the club at least sealing a third straight season in the Premier League.

The man from Trinidad enjoyed the time with Ricky as manager, but he said that the pressures of management is something he didn't want to have full time, opting for a coaching role instead.

Kenwyne said, 'Ricky came in and steadied the ship, but he always believed that management wasn't for him, we did have some fun times though.'

This would be Ricky Spragia's only period as a first-team manager. He came to Sunderland as a coach after building a successful reserve team at Manchester United, including players such as Darren Fletcher and Kieran Richardson; the latter was of course a team-mate of Kenwyne's at the Stadium of Light for several years.

His time on Sunderland started in 1994 as youth-team coach and then reserve-team coach. He left for old Trafford in 2002 and remained at Manchester United until 2007.

Spragia took over as caretaker manager at the start of December when Roy Keane was sacked, and by the end of the month he had been appointed on a permanent basis, signing an 18-month deal.

Yet following a 3-2 home defeat to Chelsea on the last day of the season, which was of no consequence as results elsewhere secured Sunderland's safety, Ricky resigned as manager. The Scotsman stayed on at Sunderland as chief scout until April 2011.

During his spell at Sunderland, Kenwyne lined up alongside several other players from his part of the world. Carlos Edwards and Dwight Yorke were both signed by Roy Keane at the start of the 2006-07 season and both had relatively successful campaigns. Stern John was brought in by Keane in the January window from Coventry.

This, alongside Kenwyne who signed in the summer of 2007, would take the Trinidad continency on Wearside up to four. It's fair to say that there will never again be so many players from the Caribbean nation.

Kenwyne said that he thoroughly enjoyed playing alongside so many others from his home country, but added that he wished the quartet had stayed together for longer with the idea that they could have brought more success to Wearside.

He said, 'It's always great to play with your countrymen, but I believed that the group should've had more time together and great things would've been accomplished.'

The 2009-10 season was one of the more enjoyable seasons in the Premier League for Sunderland. Steve Bruce was appointed manager in the summer and there was a major shake up in the playing staff. Many of the players who helped get Sunderland back to the top flight, including Danny Collins, David Connolly and Carlos Edwards, were sold on.

In their place, the likes of Lee Cattermole, Lorik Cana and Darren Bent arrived. Kenwyne would go on to form a good partnership upfront with Bent and, along with another new signing Frazier Campbell, Sunderland had one of their strongest attacks in recent history. The trio scored 37 of Sunderland's 48 league goals, with Kenwyne getting nine of them.

Throughout the season, Arsenal and Liverpool came to the Stadium of Light and left empty handed, the latter being on the end of a very controversial goal which deflected in via a beachball thrown onto the pitch by Liverpool fans before kick-off.

During the season, Kenwyne found the back of the net against some of the formidable sides in the Premier League. Sunderland drew 2-2 away to Manchester United and 1-1 at home to Manchester City, with the Caribbean striker scoring in both. He would also score the third in the away match against City, although the end-to-end contest just before Christmas ended 4-3 to the hosts.

Also included in the 2009-10 season tally was the opening goal in a 2-1 away defeat to Wolverhampton Wanderers on the last day of the season, a strike that would be his last in Sunderland colours.

Kenwyne's time at Sunderland came to an end when he moved down to Stoke City before the start of the 2010-11 season. It seemed to be a move that he didn't want to make, but the relationship with then manager Steve Bruce made Kenwyne decide his future lay elsewhere.

When asked if he felt his time at Sunderland came to a natural end, Kenwyne said, 'No it didn't, I think that I should've been there at least a couple years more, but differences with the next manager proved to be too much.

'I would sum up my time as unfinished, like I said, differences between myself and the last manager from my time there were too much, so I didn't leave feeling comfortable.'

When asked what his biggest regret during his time at Sunderland was, Kenwyne said that is was how soon he left the club. It can be said that many fans would have been disappointed when he left and probably felt he had a lot more to offer Sunderland, especially as the following season Darren Bent would also depart the Stadium of Light.

Talking of regrets, Kenwyne said, 'My biggest regret is not being there longer because I really love the club.'

Kenwyne's playing career took him around the world and gave him many years in the top tier of English football.

After leaving Wearside, Kenwyne played for Stoke, Cardiff City, Bournemouth, Al Jazira in Abu Dhabi and Atlanta United in the USA. He also represented his country 82 times, including being part of Trinidad & Tobago's only appearance at a World Cup in 2006. Other members of the 'Soca Warriors' squad to travel to Germany were future Sunderland team-mates Carlos Edwards and Dwight Yorke, who captained the side. The side brought flare and charisma to the tournament but picked up just one point in a 0-0 draw against Sweden and finished bottom of their group, which also included England and Paraguay.

Kenwyne went on to score 23 goals for his country, making him Trinidad's second highest goalscorer of all time behind another former Sunderland player, Stern John. That figure will surely see him go down as a legend in Trinidad & Tobago football for years to come.

When reflecting on his career, Kenwyne said, 'My career went well in my opinion, I would like to thank all the managers that brought me to the clubs, I appreciate the experience.'

Since hanging up his boots, Kenwyne has turned to passing on his knowledge to the next generation of players. He didn't rule out a possibility of coming back to Wearside in some capacity.

'So far I'm doing some coaching, I do think I have a wealth of experience to pass on, who knows, someday I may end up coaching at Sunderland.'

Kenwyne Jones was a fan favourite at the Stadium of Light thanks to his flare and cool finishing. Injuries during his time at the club made it so his true potential was never fulfilled. As he has said, Kenwyne regrets how his time at the club ended and wished he could have spent longer on Wearside.

He is a player who could have done a lot more at Sunderland. The following season saw Sunderland really click, and even after a shaky second half of the season they finished tenth in the Premier League, their highest Premier League finish in ten years and second highest in the history of the competition.

With added goals and other contributions from the man from Trinidad, one can only wonder how much more Sunderland could have achieved. Instead, there started a gradual decline as poor decisions were made on and off the pitch.

On a personal note, the seasons Kenwyne Jones was at Sunderland was a mini golden era. The side played good football and by the time he left for Stoke he had stuck out three campaigns back in the Premier League, all three of which had their highs and lows. He was brought in by Roy Keane to fire Sunderland towards Premier League survival, and he left having helped Steve Bruce secure a comfortable 13th-place finish.

The season after Kenwyne left saw Sunderland play some of their best football in the Premier League, and it will never be known if they could have taken the extra steps towards breaking into the top ten further if he had still been part of the club.

2010-11 AND BEYOND ...

The following season would see Sunderland finish tenth, their highest finish in over ten years. The years following this would see a slow and steady decline. The cracks on the top of the club gradually made their way down into every corner.

With Sunderland, it reached a point where narrowly avoiding relegation year in, year out was deemed a success.

Other than six straight wins over arch-rivals Newcastle United and a League Cup final appearance in 2013, the decade had so far been one to forget on Wearside.

After four close shaves with relegation and no real signs of improvement, the inevitable relegation happened in 2017. Under David Moyes, Sunderland had become a side that showed little fight and almost as much ability. Relegation was confirmed with a 1-0 defeat by Bournemouth in April, ending a disappointing period in the club's history.

It was hoped that relegation to the Championship would give Sunderland a clean slate from which to build on. However, the wheels came off very quickly and the Black Cats hurtled towards a second straight relegation. In a poor bottom six, Sunderland stood out as the worst of the lot. Finishing bottom of the Championship, Sunderland dropped into the third tier of English football for only the second time in their history.

For a whole generation of Sunderland fans, the final whistle in the 2-1 defeat against Burton Albion at the Stadium of Light, which confirmed relegation to League One, was the lowest moment following their club.

It was an abysmal campaign, in which Sunderland won just seven out of 46 league games. Despite always being just a few points away from the right side of the dashed line of safety,

Sunderland were in the relegation zone from New Year's Day onwards. They dropped to bottom of the table after a 2-2 draw at Reading and remained there for the remaining four league games.

For the second summer running, a clear out was needed at the Stadium of Light. Long-term owner Ellis Short sold the club to Stewart Donald. New manager Jack Ross brought in many new players and kept faith with academy products such as Lyndon Gooch and George Honeyman, and the latter he made club captain.

The season was more enjoyable than any in the last five years in terms of watching Sunderland win matches, but most of the fans looked upon the campaign as a failure. Two Wembley finals, one in the Football League Trophy and the other in the play-off final, and two defeats meant that Sunderland had failed to gain promotion.

Despite only losing five matches, three of these in the last six, Sunderland finished the season in fifth. They became experts in drawing; 19 matches ended level, with 15 of these being 1-1. The inability to break teams down ultimately cost Sunderland promotion.

The coronavirus outbreak put a halt to the season in March, by which time Sunderland hadn't shown much improvement. The start of the season could have been worse, with one defeat in the first ten. Jack Ross was sacked in October and replaced by Phil Parkinson. A 0-0 draw at home to rock-bottom Bolton Wanderers on Boxing Day left Sunderland 15th in the League One standings. A turnaround was needed quickly.

This came in some style. In the New Year Sunderland went on to win nine games in 12, rising into fourth place. By the time football was suspended in March, Sunderland lay seventh and just a point from the play-offs.

It is at this point that Sunderland now find themselves. It's been a gradual period of decline for the club, with no one fully understanding how they can at least get back to the Championship.

Not for a very long time has being a Sunderland supporter been consistently enjoyable. It reached the point in the mid-2010s where staying up by the skin of their teeth was cause for celebration, only to fail to build on survival and go through the same ordeal 12 months later. Without real investment, this cycle is destined to continue, but at a lower level.

Sunderland could become a club that bounces between the second and third tiers of English football, but if there is a club to watch then the fans will turn up in their numbers.

At the end of the day, it is the fans who make this football club. Most of the players involved in this book acknowledge the passion and influence the supporters at Sunderland, whether at Roker Park, the Stadium of Light or in the away end of grounds in the furthest reaches of England, have for their club.

Sunderland are better off than a lot of football teams in the country, but there are likely few where the team means so much to the people. The Stadium of Light is a place many see more than a lot of their families and friends. It is near to the centre of a city that is football mad.

The club has moved to keep up with changes to the game and the wider world and it will no

doubt continue to change in the years to come. However, the recipe to be a successful player who is adored on Wearside has remained the same for decades.

For any footballers out there who may have attracted interest from Sunderland AFC, or perhaps want to know what it takes to be a success at the Stadium of Light, there isn't much to it. If you work hard on the pitch week in, week out, keep your head up, and scrap for every blade of grass, then you will be remembered well.

The players in this book are evidence of this. Many will not have played for a club as big or with as passionate supporters as Sunderland, but they remember their time on Wearside with the most fondness because they gave this attitude which all supporters want their players to show.

In the ever-changing world of football and amongst the eye-watering price tags which are thrown around, there will always be room for a player with a passionate, never-say-die attitude and a love for playing for the fans who sing their name.

The 2019-20 season was disrupted by the coronavirus pandemic, and thus Sunderland were confined to a third season in League One. A poor run before football was suspended saw the Black Cats drop out of the play-off places and League One teams voted to end the season prematurely. Sunderland lay just three points from the automatic-promotion places and ended the campaign in their worst-ever league finish in the clubs 140-year history.

Pandemic or not, Sunderland have ended on a new low for the third season in a row. Things have rarely been good for Sunderland fans, and with the news at the start of June that a third straight season in the third tier was on the cards this doesn't look like it will change any time soon.

With promotions and play-offs going ahead, as well as the continuation of the Championship season, Sunderland will be in a division with seven new and hungry sides; all of which will be looking to take the scalp of the Black Cats.

Four years ago, Sunderland were facing up to Manchester City, Liverpool and Chelsea. Starting the 2020-21 campaign they will be locking horns with teams such as Crew Alexandra, Swindon and Plymouth Argyle. With the greatest respect to those teams, it is a monumental fall from grace for Sunderland. However, it is one that has been likely since long before relegation from the top flight in March 2017.

Sunderland Association Football Club is on a hiding to nothing, and they probably always will be, but as long as the club continues to exist they will continue to be followed by some of the most loyal supporters in the game. If the day comes that someone enters the club and turns it around, they will be treated with God-like admiration across Wearside.

Printed in Great Britain
by Amazon

50352256R00111